IN THE SKIES OVER EUROPE

IN THE SKIES OVER EUROPE

The Memoirs of Luftwaffe Fighter Pilot Günther Scholz

from the Legion Condor to the Defense of the Reich

Ingo Möbius

Translated from the German by David Johnston

Schiffer Military History
Atglen, PA

Originally published as,
Im Einsatz über Europa: Der Jagdflieger Günther Scholz erinnert sich,
by Eigenverlag Ingo Möbius, Chemnitz, 2009.

Book design by Robert Biondi.

Library of Congress Catalog Number: 2010941407.

Printed in China.
ISBN: 978-0-7643-3760-4

We are always looking for people to write books on new and related subjects. If you have an idea for a book, please contact us at the address below.

Published by Schiffer Publishing Ltd.
4880 Lower Valley Road
Atglen, PA 19310
Phone: (610) 593-1777
FAX: (610) 593-2002
E-mail: Info@schifferbooks.com.
Visit our web site at: www.schifferbooks.com
Please write for a free catalog.
This book may be purchased from the publisher.
Please include $5.00 postage.
Try your bookstore first.

In Europe, Schiffer books are distributed by:
Bushwood Books
6 Marksbury Ave.
Kew Gardens, Surrey TW9 4JF
England
Phone: 44 (0)20 8392-8585
FAX: 44 (0)20 8392-9876
E-mail: info@bushwoodbooks.co.uk
www.bushwoodbooks.co.uk

CONTENTS

PREFACE

A fighter pilot's success is usually measured by the number of his victories. During the Second World War there was a large circle of extremely successful pilots within the German Air Force. Of these, 107 achieved more than 100 confirmed victories.

Because of their military success, they were awarded the highest decorations and achieved rapid promotion. They rose to command operational units and reached the highest levels of command within the Luftwaffe.

There were, however, also fighter pilots who enjoyed impressive careers without achieving high victory totals, men such as Eduard Neumann, Walter Stengel and Gotthard Handrick. Their qualities lay more in commanding the units and soldiers entrusted to them rather than ambition to increase their own victory tally. Today former members of the Luftwaffe still speak with the highest respect about their former superiors. Among the names that are mentioned is that of Günther Scholz.

In this book Scholz recalls the early years of the Luftwaffe and his time in Spain as a member of the "Legion Condor", where he gained his first combat experience at the side of Adolf Galland and Werner Mölders. He tells of his actions as a *Staffelkapitän* over Poland and France, during operations against Great Britain, over Russia and in Yugoslavia. Scholz describes his time as *Gruppenkommandeur* and *Geschwaderkommodore* on the Polar Sea Front and his final post of *Jagdfliegerführer* in Norway.

The reader must bear in mind, however, that a considerable period of time has elapsed since the events described herein took place. It makes no claims to being a gapless biography or even a military-historical documentation of the events of those days. As well, no attempt was made to detail individual combats and provide gripping descriptions of them. The book is, however, enriched by numerous photographs.

Günther Scholz had no personal documents such as a diary or logbook on which he could base his account. Special appreciation is therefore given to Christian Kirsch of Berlin for making available his personal resources on JG 54 in general and Max-Hellmuth Ostermann in particular.

I also wish to thank all those other persons who helped in the creation of this book.

Ingo Möbius
Chemnitz, May 2009

INTRODUCTION

Günther Scholz was one of the most outstanding fighter commanders to serve Germany during the Second World War. When I met him, we were both enjoying a wonderful time as pilots in beautiful East Prussia. No one was thinking of war. We young pilots admired the older, more experienced pilots such as Günther Scholz. As *Staffelkapitän*, he was our role model both as a pilot and a military man.

At that time Günther Scholz had been transferred to the military base at Gutenfeld near Königsberg for the formation of a new fighter *Gruppe*. This *Gruppe* later became part of JG 54, the famous Green Heart *Geschwader*. The fighter units were equipped with the proven Me 109 fighter aircraft. Günther Scholz was not only an outstanding pilot, but also a circumspect leader who cared about the welfare of his men.

During the war, these qualities caused him to rise rapidly to senior command positions, first as *Gruppenkommandeur* and later *Geschwaderkommodore* in JG 5, the famous *Eismeergeschwader*, in Finland.

As a result of our time together in JG 5 and the experiences we shared, Günther Scholz and I formed a friendship that has lasted until the present day.

Hans-Ekkehard Bob
April 2009

1
Road to the Luftwaffe

"I was born in Breslau on 8 December 1911. My father held a degree in engineering and was an engineer with the Breslau Fire-Brigade. He fought in the First World War, but because of his activities as a firefighter he was not inducted until 1916. He joined the pioneers and spent the war on the Western Front as a flamethrower operator.

I grew up in a Breslau fire hall, an interesting place for a boy. There was, for example, a large room, the so-called telegraph room. That is where all the calls came in as to where there was a fire or where the fire brigade was needed. We boys waited outside this room, and whenever something interesting started happening we grabbed our bicycles and followed the fire brigade to the scene of the fire.

In 1927 my father applied for and won the position of director with a fire insurance company. He went from being an official with the fire brigade to an employee of an insurance company. For the family this meant a move to Magdeburg and for me a change of schools, which resulted in me being put back a year. I graduated from secondary school in Magdeburg.

The insurance company gave my father the task of improving the organization of the volunteer fire brigades in the towns and small cities of the so-called Province of Saxony. Most of these brigades were equipped with outmoded equipment. Magdeburg was the capital city of Saxony; the present-day state of Saxony-Anhalt did not then exist.

My father spent most of the week in his car, travelling throughout the province and organizing the volunteer fire brigades. These could not afford expensive fire trucks like the fire brigades in the big cities. Instead they had pumps powered by DKW motorcycle engines, which they placed on trucks for transport to the fire. When they arrived on the scene, they fired up the pump's engine, which enabled them to operate two to three hoses.

One of the firms that built the pumps and associated suction apparatus was the Flader Company of Jöhstadt in the Erz Mountains. Because of the business dealings between my father and the company, a friendship soon developed with the Flader family. Now and again my parents and I were invited to Jöhstadt. *Herr* Flader was already an older man and his wife was quite a bit younger. He died after some time and *Frau* Flader took over the running of the company. To me she became Aunt Flader. In winter I often travelled alone to Jöhstadt to ski and lived in the family home.

I was excited about flying even as a youth. It was the stories and the reading of books that awakened my interest in aviation. When I graduated from school, my father granted my wish to join the *Deutsche Luftsportverband** and earn my pilot's license. Thus my career as a pilot began in 1933." (**Deutsche Luftsportverband*: an organization set up by the Nazi Party in March 1933 to establish a uniform basis for the training of military pilots. It was dissolved in 1937 and replaced with the National Socialist Flyers Corps, a corporation under public law and subordinate to *Reichsluftfahrtminister* Hermann Göring.)

During the First World War, aviation units had played an important role in warfare for the first time in history. Aircraft development progressed rapidly during the four years of war. After the end of the war in 1918 and the Versailles Treaty of 1919, Germany was forbidden to have an air force. The German military aviation units were disbanded on 8 May 1920 and their remaining aircraft were either handed over to the Allies or destroyed.

The strict terms of the Versailles Treaty also placed restrictions on Germany with respect to the development of new aircraft. Not until 21 May 1926, when the Paris Aviation Agreement was signed, were these restrictions lifted. From that point onward, Germany was at least permitted to engage in civil aviation without excessive restrictions.

At the same time, the *Reichswehr* bypassed the restrictions of the Versailles Treaty by training a small number of pilots at civilian establishments, such as the German Commercial Pilot's School founded in 1927. The best of these were sent to Russia for further training. As the result of a secret agreement signed in the early 1920s, in 1925 Germany established a secret flying school at Lipetsk. A number of very well known names in the Luftwaffe received their first fighter training there.

On 30 January 1933 Adolf Hitler was named chancellor of Germany. The National-Socialists intensified the efforts begun by the *Reichswehr* for a new German air force. The German Sports Flying Association was formed on 25 March 1933. In it were combined all civilian and paramilitary units, clubs and organizations associated with aviation. The DLV thus became an important building block for a new air force. Placed in charge of the organization was Bruno Loerzer, a famous fighter pilot from the First World War and a wearer of the *Pour le Mérite*.

"The DLV was officially a civilian institution and one had to pay to earn one's pilot's license. I wanted a career as an engineer, like my father, and I had applied for admission to the technical academy in Hanover. Before I could begin my studies

I had to be able to show a year's practical experience. After graduation, therefore, I spent a year as a trainee with Krupp-Gruson in Magdeburg.

And so I worked all day and in the evenings went to the Magdeburg airport. The weekends were also dedicated to flying. I made my first flights with an instructor in a Klemm two-seater. The instructor sat up front and I, with the stick in my hand, behind him. As a precaution, there was another stick in the front cockpit so that the instructor could intervene in an emergency.

At first we flew circuits and practiced landings. There was also a great deal of theory to be learned. The entire training program lasted about a month. Then it was time for my test and the A2 certificate beckoned. In order to obtain this basic pilot's license, one had to fly a circuit solo and successfully complete a short cross-country flight. Once this was completed, the next step was simple aerobatics.

Aerobatics training was carried out in the Bücker Jungmann. Whereas the Klemm was a low-wing monoplane made of plywood, the Bücker Jungmann was a fabric-covered biplane. If one completed these flights successfully, one was issued the A2-Land pilot's license.

I have many pleasant memories of my time at the DLV. Back then they wanted to interest the German people in aviation, and there was not yet a German air force. The so-called Germany Flights were organized for this purpose. They were sort of an advertisement for aviation. One flew across the country to other airfields as part of a group of machines. Air days were organized at the airfields. We young pilots took part in these events and gave short aerobatic displays or flew in formations with several other aircraft.

Before long one began hearing rumors about the coming of a new German air force. They were already recruiting for it. Officially, in keeping with the terms of the Versailles Treaty, Germany was forbidden an air force, but it appeared that a secret buildup was already under way. As I mentioned, by then I had applied for enrollment in an engineering program in Hanover. I had few illusions about my subsequent prospects, however. The number of unemployed had reached its peak in Germany in 1932. There had been a change of government and the numbers were dropping, but there was no way of predicting how quickly this would affect the labor market. What good was a degree if I ended up unemployed?

By then there was constant talk of a coming new air force with wonderful new machines. Why not make a career of flying then? And so I volunteered for the still-secret Luftwaffe. My decision had been made. I wanted to become an officer."

On 27 April 1933, Hermann Göring, wearer of the *Pour-le-Mérite* and follower of Adolf Hitler, was named State Minister of Aviation. At the same time, plan-

ning for a new air force was begun. Officially nothing was said about it, for the restrictions of the Versailles Treaty were still in force, even though the *Reichswehr* had long ago begun exceeding its authorized strength. Germany was still forbidden to have an independent air force, but for how much longer?

The training of German pilots in Russia ended and began taking place in Germany itself. The first aviation units were formed under cover designations. The new air force would also need young officers. They would be trained by the army and navy. At the beginning of 1934 Günther Scholz decided to take this path.

"The future air force officers were trained by the navy at Stralsund and the army at Dresden. At the beginning of April 1934 I received my call-up papers with orders to report to Stralsund. Altogether, there were 180 officer candidates there. All wanted to join the future air force.

First, however, there was basic training. This we received from 8 April to 13 June 1934 on the island of Dänenholm near Stralsund with the 6th Company of the II Battalion of the Baltic Ship's Cadre Division.

This was followed by training at the naval schools in Mürwick and Flensburg. On 15 June 1934, one day after our arrival, we became sea cadets and had thus climbed the first step of the career ladder.

We studied theory at Mürwick, but it was all dedicated to the navy. For example, we learned the rules of the sea, even though it had nothing at all to do with the air force. We also practiced tying the various kinds of navy knots. Then there was sailing instruction.

The Mürwick Naval School was wonderfully situated, right on the Flensburg Fjord. Cutter pulling became a strenuous affair. One could say that we received proper training as seamen. On the other hand, we also had army officers, who gave us land training. That also had nothing to do with the air force. Gradually, we began asking each other when we were going to hear something about aircraft and about flying. Why, in fact, did an aircraft fly? They would have to explain it to us sometime. But there was no one there who could answer our questions. As I mentioned before, we future air force officers were trained exclusively by the army and the navy, and our lectures reflected this.

We aspiring officers also received several hours of so-called lessons in deportment. We were taught how an officer should conduct himself in civilian life. They taught us table manners, among other things. We learned how to use the many items of cutlery, when one should use which knife or which fork. They told us how many visitor cards we should request and pass out for official occasions. They also taught us that, when walking with a woman, one should always remain on the right. On the street, however, one always had to walk on the side nearest the roadway, to prevent the woman from being splashed by passing vehicles. To sum it up, these were things had never been of much interest to us before, but which the navy thought it important that we should learn.

These lessons in deportment were given by our company commander, *Kapitänleutnant* Wilhelm Bloser, at the naval school in Mürwick. To our great enjoyment, he conducted them in the most drastic manner. One day he told us that we would now learn how to and then practice kissing a woman's hand. We were told not to raise the woman's hand too far or ourselves bend too low, but most importantly we were told not to press our lips full on the hand, but instead just lightly touch it.

Our class was always divided into groups of about twenty for the seminars. *Kapitänleutnant* Bloser stood before us, and after his demonstrations would say, "Imagine that I am a woman!" Then we all had to pass by him as he held out his hand. And so we practiced hand-kissing. None of us will ever forget the scene and especially his statement, "Imagine that I am a woman!"

Kapitänleutnant Loser had been born in 1898. He joined the Imperial Navy in 1917 and served in the submarine arm during the First World War. He always wore a white handkerchief with his blue navy uniform. This fancy handkerchief was a regular trademark of his.

In the summer of 1934 our course went to the training camp at Königsbrück near Dresden for fourteen days. In addition to field exercises, we watched demonstrations by the army. There was one by an artillery battery and a smoke generator company also had to show what it could do.

For one day, however, we had to put on our best. In naval uniform, the entire class had to pay a propaganda visit to the Saxon capital. Led by a band, we marched through Dresden in formation, with *Kapitänleutnant* Bloser in the lead. It was morning, and the inner city was filled with people who stopped in astonishment and looked at us. A navy outfit so far inland was an extremely unusual sight for them.

After our march, near the opera house we turned into the "Italian Village". Once again, a crowd gathered immediately. They weren't allowed into the beer garden, however, for otherwise we wouldn't have been able to eat in peace. I have fond memories of our days in Königsbrück, for several times during this period we were able to get to know Dresden after we were off duty. The condition that we had to do so in naval uniform brought us many invitations.

Our time in Mürwick lasted until 31 March 1935. By then I had been promoted to *Obermatrose* on 1 October 1934 and *Oberstabsmatrose* on 1 January 1935. I subsequently passed my officer candidate test and on 1 April 1935 was named *Fähnrich.*

On the same day we returned to Stralsund for a six-week platoon leader's course. Our next stop, on 15 June 1935, was the II Naval Artillery Battalion in Wilhelmshaven. As *Fähnriche*, we were now to train recruits ourselves. This was in fact an important component of the officer training program.

While we were in Wilhelmshaven we wore army uniforms, and we only put on our blue navy uniforms when we went out. Looking back, these were very interesting and informative months, for we learned for the first time to lead soldiers who had been entrusted to us. On 1 October 1935 I was promoted to *Oberfähnrich*.

Our service in the Naval Artillery Battalion ended at the end of the same month and we were discharged from the navy. One-and-a-half years had passed since I joined the service in 1934. Much had changed in Germany. Now there was officially an air force again and nothing else stood in the way of my chosen career.

My class of about 180 officer candidates was assigned to various flight training schools. We had to declare which branch of the service we wanted to serve in. I volunteered for fighter pilot training and together with thirty other comrades I was sent to Salzwedel."

2
Carefree Years

On 26 February 1935, in a decree which took effect on 1 March 1935, Hitler declared the Luftwaffe an independent element of the armed services. The period of secrecy was officially over. The first formations had already displayed themselves to the public on Reich Party Day. (National Party Congress)

Caught up in the euphoria of the buildup, on 1 November 1935 *Oberfähnrich* Scholz and about thirty others from his navy class arrived at the flight training school at Salzwedel.

"During our first months at the flight training school we still wore our blue navy uniforms. We had to have the tailor make us a blue-gray Luftwaffe uniform.

Those newcomers who did not know how to fly first had to earn their pilot's badge. I already had it and thus was able to begin type flying straight away. The school had more than twenty types of aircraft, from light training machines like the Klemm and the Bücker Jungmann to the large, multi-engine Ju 52. We each began by flying several circuits and this was followed by cross-country flights on the various types.

When all of the pilots had reached a level of competence, we were to learn to fly on instruments. The flight training school at Salzwedel had a total of two Ju 52s. Our class was divided and fifteen men boarded each of the machines. We took turns sitting at the controls in the cockpit, with the flight instructor seated beside us. Curtains blocked the pilot's view of the outside, while the instructor had a clear view. The students were supposed to fly with reference to the instruments only. Our flights from Salzwedel took us in various directions. We changed places after a certain time and the next man took his place at the controls.

Once we flew to Essen and landed at the airfield there. We had an hour to do as we pleased before the flight back to Salzwedel. Wearing our overalls, we already felt like proper Luftwaffe officers, and consequently we wanted to behave as such. The large café restaurant in the terminal building was our destination. We sat down and ordered lots of coffee and cakes. Meanwhile our aircraft was refueled and checked over.

After an hour we climbed back into our Junkers and began the return flight. My turn came to take the controls. Very soon, however, the fun of flying disappeared. The air was very turbulent. The Ju 52 flew very slowly and took each bump comfortably. All of a sudden I felt ill. I had partaken freely of the coffee in particular and had also eaten plenty of cake. Each air pocket made me feel worse. The Junkers dropped and then rose again. Each time the machine rose, the contents of my stomach did the same.

I dared not say anything to the flight instructor. I was able to keep it down a few times, but then suddenly everything erupted from me, right onto the instruments. I couldn't see a thing. Now I had no choice but to tap the pilot. He was furious at first, but what was done was done. I took my handkerchief and cleaned up the instrument panel so that I could again see something.

Sitting in the aircraft's cabin behind the cockpit, the others literally got wind of my misfortune. Perhaps some of the others had been feeling ill too, perhaps it was the smell, perhaps the notion that they would have to take another turn at the controls, but whatever the reason, several of my comrades also saw the return of their coffee and cake. The windows of the Ju 52 slid open. My comrades stuck their heads out and were sick, leaving brown stripes on the aircraft's fuselage.

The flying lesson was thus over and we headed straight to Salzwedel. After landing, the pilot declared that each one of us should chip in to compensate the ground crew who would have to clean the aircraft. That stood to reason, and each of us made a contribution. We found this all very embarrassing.

At that time *Major* Trautvetter was commander of the Salzwedel Flight Training School. He was an enthusiastic fan of popular music and also liked to drink. Often we had to sit and drink with him in the evenings, even though we were on duty the next day and would have preferred not to. But as long as the commanding officer didn't stand, we had to remain seated too."

Rudolph Trautvetter had been born in East Prussia in 1891. He had done a one-year tour as a volunteer in the Imperial Army before the First World War. During the war he had found his way to the *Fliegertruppe*, rose to become an officer and finally flew as an observer. He remained in aviation after the war. From the mid 1920s he was active at a variety of civilian flying schools until, on 1 May 1934, he put on the uniform again as a *Hauptmann*. His first posts were the flight training schools at Würzburg and Fürth. On 1 April 1935 he was named commander of Flight Training School Salzwedel and on 1 September was promoted to *Major*.

In the ten years to come, Trautvetter remained in the Luftwaffe's training organization, rose to the rank of *Generalmajor* and on 26 March 1944 was awarded the German Cross in Silver for his service. Based on current knowledge, this decoration was only awarded sixty times to members of the Luftwaffe.

"I was promoted to *Leutnant* on 1 April 1938. My sojourn at Salzwedel ended at the same time, and I was transferred to the newly-established *Jagdgeschwader* 232 at Bernburg near Halle. The *Geschwader* consisted of a single *Gruppe* with no *Geschwaderstab**. (**Geschwader* Headquarters) In command of this so-called *Jagdgruppe* Bernburg was *Oberst* Bruno Loerzer. It was his first post since being reactivated.

The Luftwaffe was being expanded and we were a thrown-together bunch. We young *Leutnants* were joined by others from the navy and the army and even a few from the police. The older officers, like *Oberleutnant* Schellmann, *Leutnant* Galland and *Leutnant* Radusch, came from the *Jagdgeschwader* "Richthofen" at Döberitz.

At Bernburg we learned formation flying on the Heinkel He 51 and practiced aerobatics and shooting at targets in the air and on the ground.

At that time we employed the so-called triangle formation, made up of three aircraft. A *Staffel* consisted of twelve aircraft, or four triangles. We eagerly practiced formation flying.

Our *Staffelkapitän* was *Oberleutnant* Hans-Heinrich Brustellin. One day he suddenly had the idea that we should climb through the clouds in *Staffel* formation.

We pilots had our doubts, as it would be almost impossible to see one's neighbor. Brustellin declared that we should fly in such a way as to not lose our neighbors, one should watch out for the others. In this way the formation could stay together. We just had to practice.

There was no solid cloud layer over Bernburg when we took off, but this soon changed. The clouds became so thick that one could no longer see his neighbors. The only possibility was to fly on instruments, but the Heinkel He 51 hadn't been designed for that, it was very simply equipped. We found ourselves in heavy cloud. Before long one couldn't tell which way was up or down. The formation disintegrated.

I was no longer able to see the aircraft flying next to me. I looked to the right, then back to the left. The artificial horizon on the instrument panel began to flutter. How was I to return the machine to a normal attitude without instruments? I couldn't.

The engine roared, I had to be in a dive. Suddenly it grew darker above me. I immediately realized that I was diving headlong towards the earth. Thank God I still had height and now knew my position in the air. My altitude was, I estimated, still 700 to 800 meters, which was sufficient to regain control of the aircraft and level out.

After landing, I learned that three of our pilots had not made it. Two had collided in cloud and one, it was later determined, was decapitated. The pilot sat in the open in the He 51. The two aircraft crashed near the outskirts of a village, quite close to a school. The extent of the catastrophe could have been much greater.

The third pilot probably realized too late that he was in a dive and was unable to pull out. Thus this exercise by the *Staffel* had cost the lives of three pilots: *Leutnant* Schneider, *Unteroffizier* Große and *Gefreite* Mühlmann. Funeral ceremonies were held at the airfield in the days that followed.

Staffelkapitän Brustellin shouldn't have conducted the exercise in this manner; at least he should have looked for thinner cloud cover or cancelled the exercise. In such a simple fighter aircraft one could not fly totally on instruments for long periods of time.

I had simply been lucky. If I hadn't had sufficient height, I would have crashed. When I look back on it, this was the first critical moment in my flying career, in which I could easily have been killed.

The commander of *Jagdgruppe* Bernburg, *Oberst* Bruno Loerzer, always liked having company. He often invited us to his villa, which was right on the airfield and where he lived with his wife. He had married a relatively young woman. She was the daughter of the owner of the Loeser & Wolff Company of Hamburg, a tobacco concern.

When Loerzer gave his small parties, he always invited several of us young *Leutnants* to attend. There was always something to celebrate. Our job was to dance with Frau Loerzer. That was no chore, it was a pleasure. She was quite pretty and we danced with her very often."

Born in Berlin on 22 January 1891, as commander of the *Jagdgruppe* Bernburg, Bruno Loerzer was something of a role model to the young pilots in Bernburg. Loerzer was the second most successful living German fighter pilot of the First World War, after Ernst Udet.

After leaving school, in 1911 Bruno Loerzer joined the 4th Baden Infantry Regiment "Prince Wilhelm" No. 113 garrisoned at Mülheim, Alsace as a *Fahnenjunker*. It was at that time that he met the young *Fähnrich* Hermann Göring. From then on, the lives of the two men would be closely intertwined.

Even before the outbreak of the First World War, Loerzer, since promoted to *Oberleutnant*, joined the nascent *Fliegertruppe* and began flight training. In November 1914, after completing his training, Loerzer visited his friend Göring in hospital in Freiburg. Göring, who had earned the Iron Cross, Second Class soon after the war broke out, had also applied for a transfer to the *Fliegertruppe* but had been turned down. Acting on his own authority, Loerzer immediately made Göring his observer and simply took him with him to *Feldfliegerabteilung* 25 at the front. Both men were fortunate not to find themselves facing court-martial.

Loerzer and Göring flew together on reconnaissance missions until the summer of 1915. In August 1915, after retraining as a bomber pilot, Loerzer returned to the front, and on 13 March 1916 he scored his first aerial victory. Continuing his successful ways, at the beginning of 1917 Loerzer was tasked with the formation of *Jagdstaffel* 26. He brought in his friend Göring, who by then was a qualified pilot, to serve as deputy *Staffelführer*.

***Jagdgeschwader* 3 was established in January 1918, with Bruno Loerzer as its commander. On 12 February 1918, after shooting down twenty enemy aircraft, *Oberleutnant* Loerzer was decorated with the *Pour le Mérite*. When the war ended in November 1918, his victory total stood at forty-four, putting him in seventh place on the list of German fighter aces, a position he shared with Rudolf Berthold. Hermann Göring shot down twenty-two enemy aircraft and was also awarded the *Pour le Mérite*.**

After seeing combat in the Baltic States as a member of various *Freikorps*, on 31 March 1920 *Hauptmann* Loerzer was discharged from the *Reichswehr*. The Versailles Treaty forbade Germany from having an air force. After holding jobs with several civilian concerns, including the Loeser & Wolff Tobacco

Company of Hamburg, in 1930 Loerzer became the manager of the *Deutschen Luftfahrzeughalter*. At that time he also encountered his old friend Hermann Göring once again. On 25 March 1933 Göring appointed him president of the newly established *Deutschen Luftsportverband* (DLV).

On 1 April 1935 Loerzer was reactivated as an *Oberst* in the new Luftwaffe. He assumed his first command – the *Jagdgruppe* at Bernburg – on 1 April 1936. It was then that Günther Scholz met him.

Loerzer later became a *Geschwaderkommodore* and *Inspekteur der Jagdflieger*. When the war broke out he was a *Generalmajor* and commander of the 2. *Fliegerdivision*, which he led during the campaign against Poland. He was subsequently named commander of the II. *Fliegerkorps*. On 1 January 1940, while serving in this position, Loerzer was promoted to *Generalleutnant* and on 29 May he was awarded the Knight's Cross of the Iron Cross for his success in the Western Campaign. He also led his corps during the Battle of Britain, the campaign against Russia and, from late 1941, the fighting in the Mediterranean Theater.

In February 1943 Loerzer was promoted to *Generalmajor* and named Chief of the Luftwaffe Personnel Office. He was also Chief of Personal Equipment and the Luftwaffe's National Socialist Leadership Branch. As the war went on, it became increasingly apparent that this close friend of Göring was no longer up to the tasks associated with his various positions. On 20 December 1944 he was relieved of his command. Initially transferred to the officer reserve, on 29 April 1945 he was discharged from active service.

The Loeser & Wolff Company of Hamburg has been mentioned several times. It was not without reason that the company hired Loerzer at the beginning of the 1920s. It was also there that he met the woman who would later become his wife. The firm's manager was Jacob Wolff. A Jew, he was born in 1868. Though a convinced pacifist, Wolff volunteered for the *Fliegertruppe* on 2 August 1914, one day after the First World War broke out. As the head of a large company with more than 4,000 employees, he would have been exempt from military service. As well, he was already forty-six years old, and the maximum age for service in the air corps was twenty-eight.

Wolff backed up his ambitions by purchasing his own aircraft and taking flying lessons at his own expense. He subsequently reapplied and requested that he be sent to the front as a fighter pilot. At that time fighter aircraft were flown exclusively by officers, and Wolf was a *Vizefeldwebel* of the Reserve.

Wolff was repeatedly rejected and made light of, but his persistence finally paid off. He was accepted and received further training, carrying out numerous practice flights. Despite many detours and lingering doubts on the part of his superiors, Wolff arrived at the front near Verdun in early 1916.

He took off on his first operational sortie on 31 January 1916. After almost losing his way in fog, Wolff was obliged to make a forced landing. Soon afterwards he again failed to find his way home after a sortie and Wolff was transferred to the rear. For some months he served as an acceptance pilot, test-flying new aircraft.

On 15 June 1916 Wolff risked his own life to save an *Obergefreiter* from drowning. His request for a transfer back to the front was subsequently granted and he was assigned to *Jagdstaffel* 17.

Wolff recorded one victory in August 1916 and another in September. Lacking witnesses, neither was officially confirmed, however he did gain the respect of his superiors for the first time.

The proverbial knot had been severed. During the year that followed, Jacob Wolff scored four confirmed victories, was decorated with both Iron Crosses, and as a fifty-year-old was promoted to *Leutnant der Landwehr*. During the air battle in which he scored his final victory on 27 July 1917, he crashed and was seriously injured.

In 1918, after a full recovery, Wolff returned to civilian life. He continued to support German aviation. This support included helping Bruno Loerzer by adding him to his company's payroll. In December 1916, with Loerzer's brother Fritz as observer, Wolff had survived an engagement with four French fighters near Verdun. The pair returned home in a machine shot full of holes.

This ends our excursion into the early days of aerial warfare. Now back to the year 1937 and the further expansion of the new German air force.

"The air force continued to grow, and the individual *Fliegergruppen* were ordered to release personnel to be used in the formation of additional *Gruppen*. Bernburg was to form a *Fliegergruppe* in Bad Aibling and I was one of those selected to go there.

Together with a small group of other young officers and several non-commissioned officers, in February 1937 we flew to Bad Aibling south of Munich. We had given up the He 51 some time ago and were now flying the latest Messerschmitt, the Me 109 C.

The airfield at Bad Aibling was already complete, and the hangars and other buildings were ready for use. All that was missing was the personnel. We, the advance party, were to be the cadre personnel of the new *Jagdgruppe*.

Bavaria is a very Catholic land and we sensed a certain distrust in the way we were greeted. When our soldiers walked through Aibling there was not a young woman to be seen, they had all disappeared. We soon learned why that was. From the pulpit the priest had warned the parents that they should protect their daughters from the gray wolves. He was referring to us. But the warning didn't last long; it was overcome by curiosity. When we walked through the town, now and then we saw a curtain behind the window moving. In less than four weeks they were all back, and very soon the first contacts were made between the local girls and us soldiers. The fear of the gray wolves had disappeared. And, after all, we weren't really all that wolf-like.

The new *Jagdgruppe* was officially established on 1 April 1937. It bore the name I./JG 135. Once again, this new *Geschwader* consisted of a single Gruppe with no *Geschwaderstab*. The new *Jagdgruppe's* commanding officer was *Major* Max Ibel. Born in 1896, he had served in the First World War as a pioneer and had ended up as a *Leutnant*. When the war began in 1939, Ibel was tasked with the formation of JG 27. On 22 August 1940 he was awarded the Knight's Cross for his success in the Western Campaign and over England.

The establishment of the *Jagdgruppe* was crowned with the formal opening of the airfield and a parade in Bad Aibling's market square.

The area in which the base was situated was a magnificent one, with the mountains right in front of our noses. In the summer we hiked, and I skied all winter. It was a wonderful time.

I developed a number of close friendships at Bad Aibling, with Hans Schmoller-Haldy and Dietrich Hrabak, for example. Hrabak and I already knew each other, as we had been in the same class in the navy.

Another member of the *Jagdgruppe* was the then *Oberleutnant* Hannes Trautloft. He was three months younger than I, had graduated from the commercial pilot's school in Schleißheim in 1931, and had trained at Lipetsk in Russia. Trautloft led the 1. *Staffel* at Bad Aibling. He was one of our most experienced pilots. The reason for this sparked great interest among us young fighter pilots.

The Spanish Civil War had been going on for some time. German participation there had long since ceased to be a secret, especially for a member of the air force. Trautloft had been one of the first members of the so-called "Legion Condor" and had gained a great deal of combat experience there. He had been in Spain from the end of July 1936 to the beginning of March 1937. Trautloft had scored five victories during that time.

At the beginning of 1938 I was asked if I would like to go to Spain. There was no pressure, it was completely voluntary. Almost everyone volunteered. The idea was attractive for a number of reasons. I was a young air force *Leutnant*, a new fighter pilot. The war in Spain beckoned as an adventure, an opportunity to put what I had learned to use, to try it out and to prove myself. I also recognized the possibility that it might help my career. Moreover, it was a chance to see something of the world and travel outside Germany, which in those days was restricted to businessmen and privileged persons. And not last, there was a huge amount of extra pay each month. These were all arguments that might convince a junior officer to accept the risks of a war deployment. My days at Bad Aibling ended on 14 February 1938."

3
In Spain

The Spanish monarchy was abolished in 1931 and the king voluntarily went into exile. The country was not prepared for the change to a democracy, however. By 1936 there had been three elections, thirty-six changes of government, numerous minor revolts and much unrest. Two political camps formed – the Nationalists on the one side and the various Republican forces on the other.

The Republican left joined with the political center. The resulting Popular Front won a parliamentary majority in the election on 16 February 1936. Some extreme leftists, believing their moment had come, called for a proletarian revolution. From that moment, Spain irrevocably sank into anarchy. Several Nationalist politicians were murdered. Fearing a reaction from the military, the Republicans abruptly disbanded the army's most important units, neutralized generals they viewed as unreliable and formed their own workers militias.

One of these generals was Francisco Franco, then forty-three years old. On 17 July 1936 he fled from exile on the Canary Islands to Spanish Morocco. The majority of the units there were on the side of the Nationalists, and Franco assumed command of them.

On 19 July 1936 the garrisons in the largest cities on the Spanish mainland began to mutiny. This uprising was brutally suppressed by the Republicans and the majority of the Spanish officer corps was eliminated. The situation in Spain had at last escalated into war.

Madrid, Barcelona and large parts of the country were in the hands of the Republicans. The Nationalists defended themselves in the south and northwest and in smaller bastions scattered throughout the entire nation.

Franco wanted to come to the aid of the Nationalists on the mainland with his units in Morocco, but the Republican navy controlled the sea route. On 26 July 1936, therefore, he sent three emissaries to Germany. They met with Hitler, who was attending the Wagner Festival in Bayreuth, and asked for his help. The Spaniards requested transport aircraft and crews. German

assistance began that same day. On 27 July the first Ju 52 flew from Berlin to Tetuan in Morocco, and soon afterwards the number of transport aircraft rose to ten.

With their help, Franco succeeded in transporting a total of 14,000 troops from Morocco to the Spanish mainland, where they joined the fighting. He assumed overall command of all Nationalist troops, which significantly strengthened their positions. Franco succeeded in gaining control of much of southern Spain and linking up with Nationalist forces in the north of the country. In November 1936 Franco and his troops reached the southern outskirts of Madrid, beginning a siege that was to last twenty-eight months. After extremely bitter fighting, at the end of 1937 the Republicans also lost control of northern Spain. At the beginning of 1938 Spain was split into a Nationalist western portion and a Republican east.

By then the Spanish Civil War had long since become a European proxy war. From the first German aid had grown the "Legion Condor", which played a decisive part in the fighting in Spain. Soon after the outbreak of war, Mussolini had also declared his willingness to help Franco. Unlike Germany, Italy sent regular army units to Spain. Republican Spain, or the Red-Spanish side as it was called, received massive military assistance, especially from the Soviet Union and France.

Officially, Germany played no part in the fighting in Spain. The "Legion Condor" was made up of volunteers, mainly from the army and air force. By the beginning of 1938 its existence was no longer a secret, especially within the ranks of the air force. For about a year and a half, men had been simply been disappearing without a trace. When they reappeared just as suddenly, they had the most terrific stories to tell. New volunteers were also sought to serve in Spain. Günther Scholz volunteered with several other members of the Bad Aibling *Jagdgruppe*.

"On 14 February 1938 those of us who had volunteered to serve in Spain were ordered to Bernburg. There had been some changes in Bernburg since my service there. *Jagdgeschwader* 232 had become *Jagdgeschwader* 137, but it still consisted of just a single *Gruppe*.

The so-called 10. *Staffel* was the preparation unit for Spain. It was attached to the *Jagdgruppe* Bernburg. The pilots destined for Spain were sent there for about fourteen days. Pilots back from Spain described their experiences in aerial combat. Maps were provided to familiarize us with Spanish geography and we were taught to identify the different types of enemy aircraft. In addition to the classroom, we also carried out practical exercises. We practiced air combat maneuvers on the Me 109 and low-level attacks on the He 51.

On a rainy morning on 2 March 1938 a group of civilians met at Berlin-Staaken and boarded a Lufthansa Ju 52 as passengers.

These civilians were fighter pilots on their way to Spain. We flew non-stop from Berlin to Rome. We landed at the Italian capital at about 14:00 hours. Taxis were waiting to take us to a hotel. An air force office had been set up in the hotel, and each man was issued 300 pesetas. We also received 100 lira for our stay in Rome.

During a brief stroll through the Italian capital we came to a square filled to overflowing. Mussolini was giving one of his too-long speeches from a balcony. Simply leaving was out of the question, for as soon as Mussolini began speaking party troops took up position at the exits from the square. We didn't understand much of the speech and would have rather have seen Rome.

At 10:00 hours the next morning we took off for Seville. The flight took us straight across the Mediterranean. These flights were always made by two aircraft, which remained in visual contact. One transport machine had gone missing. The cause remained a mystery, but it was suspected that Red fighters had shot it down over the Spanish coast.

We landed at Seville in magnificent spring weather. In Berlin it was still almost winter. We were driven to the Hotel Christina. The next morning we were supposed to fly on to Burgos in a mail aircraft, departure time 06:30.

That night I spent 200 of my 300 pesetas in Seville. With throbbing heads and dead tired, at 06:30 we took off for Burgos. The city was the seat of the Franco government. Madrid was still in the hands of the rojos, the Reds.

In Burgos we were issued Spanish uniforms. In Spain we were upped one step in rank, and I became an *Oberleutnant*. The next day a communications aircraft of the German legion's fighter unit flew us to Saragossa-San Jurga.

The "Legion Condor" was made up of units from all three branches of the *Wehrmacht*. The air force contributed a fighter group, a bomber group, a dive-bomber group, a reconnaissance group with tactical and strategic reconnaissance machines, and a maritime reconnaissance group. There was also a flak regiment, which operated in the air defense and ground support roles, two signals regiments and supply units. Personnel, equipment and aircraft were regularly sent from Germany.

Non-commissioned officers and enlisted men served nine months on average. Officers were relieved after a year. Each soldier continued to be paid in Germany. In Spain we received so-called "danger pay", which was based on one's rank and type of duty. Pilots received more than the ground personnel, for example.

This pay was very high, and for a *Leutnant* pilot like me it was 1,200 *Reichsmark* per month. Half of this I received in pesetas, while the other half was deposited into a savings account in Germany. A flying *Leutnant* thus received a total remuneration of 1,500 *Reichsmark*. Money was not a problem for those returning home from Spain.

At that time 100 pesetas was equal to about 30 *Reichsmark*. Our pay was thus equivalent to 2,000 pesetas. One could live like a king on that sum. Most of those who served in Spain went home with 9,000 to 10,000 *Reichsmark* and the first thing they did was purchase an automobile.

In later years I asked myself where all this money for the German troops in Spain had come from. It was indirectly paid by Franco. He in turn received it from England, America and the Vatican. Red Spain, on the other hand, received support from Communist Russia in the form of weapons and personnel and volunteer units from the Communist parties of every nation. There were even Germans fighting on that side.

The Spanish Civil War was practically the first conflict between capitalism and communism, with Hitler and Mussolini occupying a hermaphroditic position. Communism – the common enemy – offset the differences between democracy and dictatorship – but only with respect to Spain and only for the duration of the war. The democracies sent no men or materiel to help Franco, but they remained benevolently neutral and kept track of the communist volunteers sent to Spain from their countries.

At that time the Legion's fighter group was commanded by *Hauptmann* Gotthard Handrick, winner of the Gold Medal in the modern pentathlon at the 1936 Olympic Games. The *Gruppe* consisted of four *Staffeln* and a headquarters company. The 1. and 2. *Staffel* were fighter units flying the Me 109. The 3. and 4. *Staffel* were ground attack units equipped with He 51s.

All newcomers were initially assigned to the ground-attack *Staffel* commanded by *Oberleutnant* Adolf Galland. It was designated 3./J 88."

Günther Scholz knew his *Staffelkapitän* from their time together in the *Jagdgruppe* Bernburg. Born on 19 March 1912, Galland became an enthusiastic glider pilot and made his way to the Luftwaffe via the commercial pilot's school. He had been in Spain since 8 May 1937. He flew his first close-support sorties in June and soon afterwards took command of the *Jagdgruppe's* 3. *Staffel*, the so-called "Mickey Mouse *Staffel*", named after its *Staffel* emblem. Galland continued to use this emblem as his career progressed.

The war took a decisive turn at the time that Günther Scholz arrived in Spain. Franco was planning an offensive in the area between Teruel and Zaragoza with the objective of breaking through to the Mediterranean at Tortosa at the mouth of the Ebro. The front about twenty kilometers southeast of Saragossa on both side of the Ebro Valley had remained almost unchanged

since 1936. The Republican front was well fortified and would not be easy to pierce.

The attack began on 9 March 1938. The entire "Legion Condor" was committed. Nationalist troops achieved important successes on the very first day. In a matter of days the penetration of the Republican positions became a breakthrough to the Mediterranean. Huesca fell on 25 March 1938, Lerida on 2 April and the port city of Vinaros was taken on 15 April. Red Spain had been split in two and Barcelona and Madrid separated.

Under Adolf Galland, the 3. *Staffel* was in action almost constantly, flying ground-attack sorties in support of the ground troops. Günther Scholz flew his first combat missions during the breakthrough.

"By then the He 51 was already obsolete as a fighter aircraft and in Spain it was employed as a low-level attack aircraft. Its armament consisted of two machine-guns and six 50-kg bombs. Low-level attacks were flown against fortified enemy positions to support the land forces. We flew over the trenches, dropped our bombs and strafed with our guns. We also attacked tank concentrations. Of course we couldn't do much with our machine-guns, but now and then, with a lot of luck, a bomb blew up a tank.

We had to personally inspect the front line to imprint it in our minds, as we would be flying low-level attacks against nests of enemy resistance the same or the following day. By taking out these nests of resistance with bombs or guns, we spared the ground troops unnecessary losses, and we German airmen were much loved by the Spanish infantry."

After reaching the Mediterranean, Franco turned south to continue his march towards Valencia. This new offensive operation began on 21 April 1938. This time there was no quick breakthrough, however. The fighting was fierce and costly, including for the "Legion Condor". The weather also turned bad. 3./J 88 moved to the La Cenia airfield near the Mediterranean coast.

When they were not flying, Günther Scholz and his comrades had plenty of time to better get to know this foreign land.

"As *Staffelkapitän*, Adolf Galland was very pleasant and comradely. His hobby in those days was hunting rabbits and deer, and it remained so until the end of his life. We found it amusing. He was a passionate hunter, but he rarely came home with anything, and when he did it was an old, dried-out hare. But Galland was extremely proud of his rabbit hunting and took every opportunity to indulge his passion.

The 3. *Staffel* had a special train fitted out to accommodate the entire unit. The pilots and ground personnel lived on the train, which also housed the unit's equipment, clothing stores and quartermaster sergeant. When the *Staffel* moved, the train followed to the nearest railway station. The pilots flew their aircraft to the next airfield and the ground personnel followed in the train.

There was even a dining car where we took our meals. Two men shared a sleeping compartment. The train was said to have been Galland's idea.

The train couldn't accompany us when we moved to the Ebro Front, as several railway bridges had been blown. The train therefore had to be left behind in Caspe and was later given to the Spaniards.

Our letters home were sent to the fake address of "Max Winkler". Letters to me were addressed G. Sch., Legion Condor, J 88. They were placed inside another envelope, and the sender was "Herr Max Winkler, Berlin". Letters to the men in Spain were collected in Berlin and delivered to Spain by airmail. For an address, we in Spain also used the address in Berlin.

At Easter we were given four days leave and drove by car from Zaragoza to the Ebro Valley by way of Huesca-Jaca-Pamplona-Vitoria (Basque Province)-San Sebastian-Guernica-Bilbao-Haro-Logrono. We drove back to Zaragoza through the Rioja wine region.

Each *Staffel* was assigned an interpreter for dealings with Spanish offices, mayors, units and so on. Our interpreter's name was Löffler. He was German, but had been living in Spain for more than twenty years and owned a hotel in Madrid. His business was idle during the war and he had volunteered to serve us.

He helped us in every conceivable situation, for instance when we wanted to buy something at a market. He showed us how to choose a spiny lobster. He told us to ensure that the creature was still quite lively and clean. If they were lethargic and tired and would scarcely move, then they would taste that way too. We got to know several local delicacies and especially how to handle them.

The Spanish girls also interested us. The Spanish were unbelievably devout Catholics. We were not, at least in the opinion of the Spanish. When we were based near the Mediterranean there were dances every Sunday. Sometimes we attended. Whenever we approached a Spanish girl, we were always turned down. They simply didn't want to dance with us.

Bordellos, however, flourished in Spain. When it came to these, the Spanish were suddenly not so serious about their faith. There were so many such installations that they came to be seen as part of everyday life.

Gotthard Handrick, the commander of our *Jagdgruppe*, understood the needs of his men. He approached the owner of one of the bordellos and made an agreement with her. From then on the group had its own bordello. It was set up in a quarter near our airfield. The place had its advantages. For one, conflicts with the Spanish population were avoided, and for another, our men were protected from disease.

For the officers it meant yet another job. From then on there was the so-called OvB, or Bordello Duty Officer. On one occasion I too had to serve as the OvB.

The whole thing took place in the evening, from 18:00 until midnight at the latest. As duty officer, one had to keep watch. Anyone wanting to enter had to report to me first. Anyone with alcohol had to surrender it. The use of alcohol was strictly forbidden there. If there were cases of petty jealousy, the officer had to step in and restore order.

This is surely a minor anecdote that is perhaps not all that well known, but that's how it was. We did more than just fly.

The missions themselves, sometimes several in one day, demanded the utmost of the pilots and aircraft. The low-level missions over frontline positions were extremely dangerous and in some cases involved a lot of flying lead. Whenever we were ordered to provide direct support to the Spanish infantry, we first had to determine exactly where the front was.

One such scouting mission to the front has stuck in my memory. Our objective was an artillery battery on the southern front in the Valencia sector. On the way there, just before we reached the front line, we came under enemy artillery fire. We could hear shells coming in. One of them made such a whistling noise as it came through the air that we thought it was heading straight for our position. There was a small pit nearby and we all dove for it.

I was unlucky. The pit was surrounded by brush, and both of my legs became caught. I fell in, and the first thing to hit the ground was my head. If that wasn't bad enough, I came down face first onto a large stone. As a result, for some time I walked around with a swollen eye and one half of my face badly battered.

The shell that had caused us to take cover fell some distance from our pit. The Nationalist-Spanish battery got the worst of it and was put out of action by the enemy fire.

In the early summer, many of the officers of the *Jagdgruppe* and commander Handrick flew to Tetuan, the capital of Spain's African colonies, for a brief visit. We spent a night in the "Exelsior", a dance bar. In addition to attractive Moroccans, there were many women of all races. These included some from France, Indonesia, Malay and even Germany.

It was also not surprising that smuggling and espionage flourished in Tetuan. Money in every imaginable currency was exchanged there."

The 3. *Staffel's* commanding officer, *Oberleutnant* Adolf Galland, had been in Spain since the beginning of May 1937. On 14 April 1938 a man stepped onto Spanish soil who was destined to be his successor. He was *Oberleutnant* Werner Mölders.

Born on 18 March 1913, Mölders joined the *Reichswehr* in 1932 and began a career as an infantry officer. When the Luftwaffe was created, *Leutnant* Mölders requested a transfer there. His first attempts to realize the dream of

flying came to nothing, however, when a doctor declared him physically unfit to fly.

Mölders refused to give up his dream, however, and he realized it through stubborn determination. His last post before going to Spain was a fighter school, where he served as an instructor.

Galland briefed his successor on the conditions in Spain and Mölders flew his first sorties as a close-support pilot in the 3. *Staffel*. On 24 May 1938 Mölders took over command of the unit from Galland. The objective of the Spanish Nationalists was still Valencia, but the front was stationary. Fierce fighting raged for possession of the city of Castellon.

In the afternoon on 31 May 1938, the 3. Staffel took off on its second mission of the day. Its orders were to locate and silence an enemy battery position. The *Staffel* flew into a hail of 20mm anti-aircraft fire and *Leutnant* Losigkeit was shot down. Losigkeit baled out of his smoking machine and came down in no-man's-land. Seconds later his aircraft crashed into the side of a mountain. His comrades circled over the spot where he had come down, but they could do nothing for him. They returned to their airfield and waited for Losigkeit to make his way back to them, but they waited in vain.

Günther Scholz was unwilling to simply wait for his friend to return. Together with interpreter Löffler and two NCOs, he drove to the front to search for the missing man. At the front they worked their way forward through the rocky terrain. Red-Spanish machine-gun fire forced them to take cover in a cleft in the rocks for several hours. Nationalist troops informed them that Losigkeit had come down about 200 meters from the enemy lines and that he had been captured by an enemy patrol after the *Staffel* flew away.

***Leutnant* Fritz Losigkeit was taken prisoner by the Reds on that day, 31 May 1938. In February 1939 he escaped and subsequently managed to return to Germany. During the Second World War he rose to the rank of *Major* and became a *Geschwaderkommodore*. Losigkeit achieved sixty-eight confirmed victories and was awarded the Knight's Cross on 28 April 1945.**

3./J 88 suffered its next casualty on 2 June 1938.

"*Leutnant* Haupt was shot down during a low-level attack. Haupt was in my *Schwarm* and I saw him bale out just above the ground. The parachute came down in no-man's-land between the lines. Patrols from both sides tried to recover the pilot. As long as we had fuel, we were able to keep the Reds away from Haupt, who was squatting on the ground, apparently wounded. As soon as we landed back at our airfield, I took a car and set off for the area where he had baled out. Members of the Spanish company deployed there told me that a minor battle had developed over the airmen and that both sides had lost men. During the night, under constant danger, we made our way to the spot, only to find that Haupt had died from his serious wounds. We brought his body back with us.

Castellon, the last major town before Valencia, was taken in mid-June 1938. A bullfight was held to mark the liberation of the city and to honor Franco. It was the first bullfight in the city in more than two years. The Reds had forbidden the sport. Anyone who knows how much the Spanish love the bullfight can imagine how much the population of Castellon had missed it.

The arena was full to bursting. With the help of our skillful interpreter Löffler and many pesetas, we secured good seats right in front of the ramp. First to appear were the key riders, dressed in medieval uniforms, With much ceremony they received the key to the pen from the alcalde, or mayor of Castellon. Then they opened the pen. The bull didn't seem to have much desire to fight, for some time passed before the master of the arena snorted into the arena with a few forced leaps and pawed the sand with his front legs.

Then the picador appeared. His job was to bait the bull, which he did by jabbing the bull in the back with lances decorated with brightly-colored bands. The barbed lances stuck there, and the pain and the bright bands infuriated the bull. One couldn't really blame him.

The angrier the bull, the more excited the crowd became; the more lethargic the bull, the angrier the crowd. If the latter happened, even the picador was booed.

Then the torero appeared and, using his famous red cape, drove the bull completely out of his mind. The torero avoided the horns of the enraged bull using just slight movements of his hips.

Finally, the terrero was replaced by the matador. His job was to kill the bull through the skilled use of a short dagger. The blow had to strike the bull's heart and kill it on the spot, otherwise the matador was booed out of the arena. On the other hand, the crowd was thrilled if the dagger found its mark.

The dead bull was then dragged out of the arena in a triumphal procession. The wilder it was at the very start, the more interesting was the event and the life-threatening work of the picadors, toreros and matadors.

Personally, I did not care for these bullfights. To us it was a form of animal cruelty. On occasion, a horse was gored by the bull's horns, slitting open its entire underbelly. The horse tried to keep running, then it fell and its intestines spilled out. The animal was dragged out of the arena and a new rider entered. We couldn't understand how the Spanish population could get so excited about such a spectacle.

Another incident from that time remains in my memory. We of course followed what was happening in the world, including important sporting events. One of the most popular German athletes at that time was Max Schmeling, the former world heavyweight boxing champion. His most spectacular bout took place in New York on 19 June 1936, when he knocked out Joe Louis, the "Brown Bomber", in the twelfth round. Louis had been widely held to be unbeatable.

Now a rematch between Schmeling and Louis was scheduled to take place on 22 June 1938. Of course the fight was broadcast on the radio. Everyone was in the mess. I, however, had come down with so-called paratyphoid fever. I had eaten something somewhere and come down with terrible diarrhea and stomach cramps. While the fight was going on I was in my room in bed. I was terribly ill.

The worst thing was that my room was right next to the mess, where all the others were sitting and listening to the fight. The noise was tremendous. All I wanted was my rest, and I prayed that the fight wouldn't go twelve rounds. Then, suddenly, it was quiet, no more noise. Now what had happened?

I got up, opened the door and asked, "What's happening?" "Schmeling's been knocked out", was the answer. Max Schmeling had been beaten, knocked out in the first round. Everyone was dismayed. How could that have happened? But I, in my situation, was happy about it. Now at least I could have some peace and quiet. The crowd in the mess broke up. I went back to my bed and was able to sleep peacefully."

By then the He 51 was obsolete. Low-level attacks had become costly undertakings, as the 3. *Staffel* had recently discovered. Since taking over the unit, Mölders had repeatedly requested that his *Staffel* be reequipped with the Me 109. His request was finally granted at the beginning of July 1938.

"Now the 3. *Staffel* also received the modern Me 109. Low-level attacks were abandoned because of heavy losses.

From then on we flew escort for the bombers or fighter sweeps. We regularly became involved in air battles, something that had almost never happened in the previous months when we were a low-level attack *Staffel*.

Werner Mölders was a Catholic and a very religious man. Nowadays they call him a criminal, and not only him, but all those who fought in Spain. Mölders was no different than the rest of us. We were pilots, fighter pilots, who performed the tasks that went along with being such."

Werner Mölders scored his first victory on 15 July 1938, and his second and third followed quickly, on the 17th and 18th. At the end of July the Legion was moved to the northern front to the bend of the Ebro River. There the Republicans had launched a counteroffensive north of Tortosa. It was in that sector that Günther Scholz spent the remaining weeks of his Spanish deployment, now as a fighter pilot.

The Battle of the Ebro raged back and forth and became a battle of attrition. Both sides pumped in more and more men and materiel. Neither side achieved significant territorial gain. Lasting three-and-a-half months, the Battle of the Ebro was one of the fiercest battles of the entire war.

"Franco's best troops were in the Foreign Legion. This consisted of African troops under the command of the best Spanish officers. The soldiers were Moroccans, Kabylians, Berbers and also some Negroes.

On one occasion, a nearby battalion headquarters invited the officers of our *Staffel* to lunch. A large table had been set up in a bungalow made entirely of reeds and grass. Laid out on the table were homemade menus. The meal lasted from 12:00 to 16:00 hours.

There was plenty of table talk, due in large part to our excellent interpreter Löffler. The hospitality of the Spaniards was impeccable and even sincere. The soldiers also wanted to speak with us and we gladly conversed with members of the various African tribes who were there.

After the Foreign Legion, Franco's most elite unit was a Moroccan division. The Moroccans saw themselves as descendants of the Vandals. They were large, with narrow, sharp-featured faces, and brave soldiers. The "Moros" were not very sentimental. As faithful Moslems they shunned alcohol, but as soon as a town was taken they plundered the bars and distilleries, set up shop beside the road, and sold the liquor to the Spanish troops at high prices.

They showed little pity for the dead enemy, the "Rojos". They relieved the dead Reds of money, jewelry and gold crowns, and sold the gold in the next city. Once, at a jeweler's, I personally saw a large box of gold crowns. Some claimed that when the Moros had no time to pull out the teeth they simply took the entire head."

Under Werner Mölders, the *Jagdgruppe's* 3. *Staffel* flew daily missions during the fierce defensive battle at the Ebro. The Messerschmitts provided fighter escort for the Stukas of the German legion and for Spanish and Italian bomber squadrons. There were frequent engagements with Red Spanish units, most of which flew the Russian-made Rata fighter.

Werner Mölders was not the only member of the 3. *Staffel* to be successful in aerial combat. On 19 August 1938, west of Flix on the Ebro, Günther Scholz scored his first victory.

"The majority of the pilots who served in Spain failed to achieve a single victory, and most of those who did got one or at most two.

My victory was more a stroke of luck. Our principal opponents were the Russian Ratas. These machines were extremely maneuverable but were not as fast as the Messerschmitt. By then we had become an efficient, tight-knit *Staffel*. When we were attacked, and the Ratas usually outnumbered us, we formed a so-called defensive circle. Flying in a circle, we were able to provide mutual cover. Anyone who tried to enter the circle immediately found one of us on his tail. It was thus extremely difficult for the enemy fighters to achieve a victory.

On that day we were again attacked by a numerically superior force of Ratas. Mölders ordered us to form a defensive circle. I had the impression that our opponents were quite inexperienced. Again and again, they blithely flew into our circle and tried to shoot one of us down. In this they failed, succeeding only in placing themselves in danger.

Suddenly, I saw a Rata drop down right in front of me. It flew into the defensive circle with the intention of shooting down the man ahead of me. He was right in front of my nose, perhaps thirty meters away. I pressed the firing button and watched my explosive bullets strike home. Fatally damaged, the Rata spun down and crashed. It was no great feat. There had been no dogfight. He simply came down from above and placed himself right in front of my guns."

In the same action in which Günther Scholz scored his first victory, Werner Mölders recorded his fourth. Scholz did not have an opportunity to add to his success in Spain, for his time in that country came to a surprisingly quick end.

"The premature conclusion of my tour of duty in Spain was due to the rise in tension caused by the Sudeten crisis, which resulted in a number of men being recalled to Germany. At the end of August 1938 we travelled by rail to the north of Spain. We then sailed for home from the port of La Caruna on the Atlantic Coast. The transport ships were commercial vessels under the Panamanian flag. We sailed through the Bay of Biscay and the English Channel to Hamburg. We wore civilian clothes for the return voyage, however this had long since ceased to be necessary.

Once during our stay in Spain, for example, we had taken an excursion to the Pyrenees. On the way we were approached by a female journalist from England who addressed us in Spanish. In doing so she instantly caught us. We knew nothing of the language and, of course, she noticed this right away. She asked us bluntly if we were Germans. We just shrugged our shoulders and walked on. What else should we have done?

But our officialdom maintained the secrecy measures, even though the world had already been informed about German participation. That is why we wore civilian clothes during our trip back to Germany.

Werner Mölders remained in Spain until the beginning of November 1938. He left the theater as the most successful fighter pilot of the German "Legion Condor" with fourteen confirmed victories.

Whenever one of us shot down an enemy aircraft, on returning to base he flew a so-called "honor circuit" of the airfield while waggling his wings. Mölders always added to this, roaring low over the airfield before suddenly pulled his machine into a vertical climb and performing a spiral. He was a virtuoso pilot.

I personally tried a number of times to perform a roll, especially later in my career, but I was never able to really complete the maneuver 100 percent. The required hand movements literally had to merge with flesh and blood. In those fractions of a second there was simply no time to think about how to operate the elevator and rudder. This maneuver, which Mölders began from a low pass, left not the slightest margin for error and from that height could have cost him his life. I simply admired him."

After returning from Spain, Mölders evaluated his combat experience and played a role in introducing a new tactic for the fighter units. On 15 March 1939 he was promoted to *Hauptmann* and made a *Staffelkapitän* in *Jagdgeschwader* 53.

When the Second World War broke out, the *Geschwader* was based on the Western Front. Mölders recorded his first victory in this war on 20 September 1939. In November he was given command of the III. *Gruppe* of JG 53. By the start of the German offensive in the west in May 1940, Mölders' had raised his victory total to nine, making him the most successful German fighter pilot.

On 27 May 1940 Mölders scored his 20th victory and two days later he became the first fighter pilot to be awarded the Knight's Cross. He was himself shot down on 5 June 1940 and spent three weeks as a prisoner of the French. As soon as he returned to Germany, on 19 July 1940 Mölders was promoted to the rank of *Major*.

One week later Mölders took over JG 51 as *Kommodore*. That same day he was shot down again, this time over the Channel, but managed to nurse his machine back to the French coast. He subsequently spent four weeks in hospital.

By 20 September 1940, during the fighting over the Channel and the so-called Battle of Britain, Mölders raised his victory total to forty. One day later he became the second soldier of the *Wehrmacht* to be decorated with the Oak Leaves and was simultaneously promoted to *Oberstleutnant*. By 8 May 1941 Mölders had raised his victory total to sixty-eight.

Mölders and his *Geschwader* subsequently moved east to take part in the attack on Russia, which began on 22 June 1941. He added four more victories on the first day of the campaign and became the second recipient of the Knight's Cross with Swords. The victories came quickly, and on 30 June 1941 Mölders equaled Manfred *Freiherr* von Richthofen's mark of eighty victories from the First World War. By 15 July his total had climbed to 101, making him the first fighter pilot in history to surpass the 100 victory mark. Combined with his fourteen victories from Spain, Mölders' total stood at 115 confirmed victories.

On that same 15 July 1941, Werner Mölders became the first German soldier to be decorated with the Knight's Cross with Diamonds. With the decoration came a ban on further combat flying. Soon afterwards, Mölders was promoted to *Oberst* and in September 1941 he was named *General der Jagdflieger*.

On 22 November 1941 the life of this successful fighter pilot came to a sudden end. Werner Mölders was on his way to Berlin to attend the funeral of Ernst Udet, who had committed suicide. The aircraft in which Mölders was flying crashed in bad weather not far from Breslau, and the young *General der Jagdflieger* was killed.

Adolf Galland, whom Werner Mölders had relieved as *Staffelkapitän* in Spain, enjoyed an equally meteoric career. After returning from Spain, like Mölders he allowed his experiences as a close-support pilot to flow into the expanding Luftwaffe. When the war broke out, Galland again saw action as a close-support pilot, over Poland. On 1 October 1939 he was promoted to *Hauptmann* and in February 1940 his request for a transfer to the fighter arm was finally granted. Galland joined *Jagdgeschwader* 27.

Galland scored his first two victories on 12 May 1940. On 6 June 1940 he was named *Kommandeur* of the III. *Gruppe* of *Jagdgeschwader* 26. By the end of the Western Campaign his victory total had risen to fourteen. Galland was promoted to *Major* on 18 July 1940 and on 29 July, after three more victories, he became the third fighter pilot to be decorated with the Knight's Cross.

Galland and Mölders were now the leading German fighter pilots, and the two friends began a fierce competition for top spot. On 23 September 1940 Galland scored his 40th victory, three days after Mölders. Like Mölders, he was awarded the Knight's Cross with Oak Leaves.

Galland was awarded the Knight's Cross with Swords on 21 June 1940, one day before Mölders, becoming the first soldier of the *Wehrmacht* to receive the decoration. On 22 August 1940 Galland was named *Kommodore* of JG 26 and on 1 November was promoted to *Oberstleutnant*. When the war in the east

began, JG 26 remained on the Channel Coast. Galland had raised his victory total to ninety-six by the time Mölders was killed. After Mölders' death Galland, who had been promoted to *Oberst* a few days earlier, was named *General der Jagdflieger*. On 28 January 1942 he was decorated with the Knight's Cross with Diamonds.

Galland remained in his new position until the beginning of 1945 and was promoted to *Generalmajor* and *Generalleutnant*. During the final months of the war he formed *Jagdverband* 44 and scored several more victories while flying the Me 262 jet fighter, increasing his victory total to 104.

Even discounting the participation of Germany and Italy, the Spanish Civil War was hardly a purely internal Spanish conflict. A glance at the list of the most successful fighter pilots from this war will suffice to confirm this.

The leading Nationalist fighter pilot was Joaquin Morato. With forty confirmed victories, he was the top scoring fighter pilot of the Spanish Civil War. Morato did not live to see the end of the war, as he was killed on 4 April 1939. As previously mentioned, Werner Mölders led the fighter pilots of the "Legion Condor" with fourteen victories. The top Italian ace was Mario Bonzano with fifteen.

The most successful Republican Spanish fighter pilot was Manuel Claver, with twenty-three victories. High on the list are two Russians, Lev Shestakov with thirty-nine victories and Sergey Gritsevets with thirty. The latest research places these figures much lower, however. Other successful Red fighter pilots included the Belgian Rudolphe de Henricourt and the Frenchman Abel Guides with ten each, the American Frank Glasgow Tinker with eight and the Czech Jan Ferâk with seven confirmed victories.

4
East Prussia

After returning from Spain and a few days leave, on 11 September 1938 *Leutnant* Günther Scholz was transferred to the *Jagdgruppe* Jesau, or the I. *Gruppe* of *Jagdgeschwader* 131, in East Prussia.

Since coming to power in January 1933, Hitler had been undoing or neutralizing the Versailles Treaty piece by piece. In addition to the restrictions imposed upon the German military, increasingly this also applied to the

territorial changes made to the borders of the European states after the First World War. It had begun with the total reincorporation of the demilitarized Rhineland in 1935 and reached a temporary climax in March 1938 when Austria was merged with Germany.

The multi-racial state of Czechoslovakia had been formed after the dissolution of Austria-Hungary in 1918. In addition to the Czech and Slovakian ethnic groups, the new state's population included a German minority of 3.5 million persons living in Bohemia, Moravia and Austrian-Silesia. Later, these territories came to be known collectively as the Sudetenland. The victorious powers officially recognized Czechoslovakia and its borders in the Treaty of Saint-Germain in September 1919.

After the integration of Austria, Hitler turned to the question of the Sudetenland. The majority of the German-speaking population did not feel part of Czechoslovakia. Hitler was determined to add the territory to the German Reich, but this time it did not look as if it could be accomplished peacefully. Czechoslovakia had no intention of yielding to Hitler's demands and it counted on the support of France and Great Britain.

In the late summer of 1938 this dispute in Central Europe seemed to be coming to a head. This was why Günther Scholz and other German volunteers in Spain were called home before their tours of duty were over. If war broke out, the air force would need experienced airmen.

In mid-September 1938 the *Jagdgruppe* Jesau was moved from East Prussia to the Nieder-Ellgut airfield near Oppeln in Upper Silesia.

"The officers of the *Jagdgruppe* Jesau were quartered in Buchenhöh Castle owned by Countess von Sierstorff. The count himself was away. All was still very peaceful. On various occasions, dinner for example, other guests were invited from the area surrounding Buchenhöh Castle, including many members of the aristocracy. They in turn invited us officers to dine with them. In this way we met two young women from the Praschma family. They invited me and another officer to dine at their parents' house the next evening.

When we arrived there we were not received by the master of the house himself or his daughters, but by the butler. He left us waiting in a sort of anteroom for quite a long time. Then one of the daughters came. She apologized for keeping us waiting and then introduced us to her father. The count was wearing a smoking outfit, more precisely just the jacket and a black bow tie. He also had on short leather pants. There certainly weren't any dress regulations.

Then we were invited in to dinner. On the way we passed through two large rooms which were completely empty. A table was set in the third room. We were invited to sit down. At table with the count were his wife and two daughters. The butler flitted about the table, looking at us with mistrust, one could even say malice.

At the end of the first course he snatched our plates away so abruptly that the silverware lying on them fell onto the white tablecloth. I looked at my companion, but said nothing. The masters of the house also said nothing. After we had finished the main course, the game continued. Again he snatched our plates away so abruptly that the knives and forks landed on the tablecloth.

When the butler had left the room, the lady of the house said, "You must forgive his conduct. Sometimes he is very willful. He opposes Hitler and hates everyone who wears a uniform." She said this very frankly and confidentially. She had no idea of our leanings, but she seemed to sense that we were not dedicated party members.

The rest of the evening was thoroughly pleasant. Later we had an opportunity to inquire about the Praschma family and learned that they were completely impoverished landed gentry. The count had sold all of his valuables and much of his furniture. Then we understood why many of the rooms had been empty."

The *Jagdgruppe* Jesau spent about 14 days in Upper Silesia, where its activities were completely routine. Meanwhile, the crisis in Europe was resolved without war. The so-called Munich Agreement was signed on 30 September 1938. Through the good offices of Italian head of state Mussolini, the leaders of the British and French governments had come to Germany. Czechoslovakia played no part in the negotiations. Hitler's territorial demands were acceded to in order to secure peace in Europe. German forces began entering the Sudetenland on 1 October 1938. Units of the air force also took part.

"Our *Jagdgruppe* moved from the forward airfield at Nieder-Ellgut to Mährisch-Trübau. The flying personnel were the first to arrive, with the ground personnel following several days later.

The population in this region was almost exclusively German. There were no sleeping quarters on the airfield itself, therefore we were billeted in private quarters. Our deployment was a short one, however, and we soon returned to East Prussia.

Because of my service in Spain, I received early promotion to *Oberleutnant*, with an effective date of 1 October 1938. Before leaving for Spain I had set up a bank account, into which my pay was deposited while I was there. Like most of my comrades, I used the money I had saved to buy an automobile. I decided on a sports car and bought a used Hansa for about 4,000 *Reichsmark*.

There were also changes in my private life. I have already spoken about the Flader family in Jöhstadt. During my time as an officer candidate, my parents and

I returned to visit the Erz Mountains. Aunt Flader told us that she had received an invitation from a family in Chemnitz, friends of hers, and that we could all go visit together. My parents agreed.

On arriving in Chemnitz, we were greeted by two young women, the daughters of the house. During the visit I struck up a conversation with the older of the girls. This acquaintanceship grew, first into friendship and ultimately into love.

Now and then during my time in Bernburg as a junior *Leutnant* pilot, my official duties took me to Leipzig or Munich. Quite often on such occasions, I took the opportunity to make a brief side-trip to Chemnitz. The city had a small airport. Once I landed there in a Me 108, another time in a He 51. For such a small airport, this was of course something of an event. I parked my aircraft and went to visit my girlfriend. I returned one or two hours later, climbed into my machine and continued my journey. At that time they tended to look the other way about such things. Of course one did have to check in and sign off with the tower. They were also able to provide the latest weather reports.

I can only characterize my time in East Prussia as pleasant. The country was magnificent and the people were very patriotic, despite their physical separation from the rest of the Reich. In order to drive from Germany to East Prussia one had to pass through the so-called Polish Corridor. The East Prussians were therefore very enthusiastic about the strengthening of the German military in their land. We were also very well received by the big land owners, from whom we received numerous invitations.

Commanding the *Jagdgruppe* at Jesau, I./JG 130 as of 1 November 1938, was the then Major Bernhard Woldenga. He had come to the air force from the merchant marine.

In those days there was one thing about which Woldenga was very passionate, and that was the fund-raising efforts of the Winter Relief Organization. We even staged an event at our airfield. One of the large aircraft hangars was cleared out and various booths were set up, for example small-caliber shooting ranges. Some of our soldiers also gave performances. It was amazing to see the talented people that emerged from our midst, from excellent piano and violin players to artists of various kinds. One man, for example, climbed a ladder made of sharp scythe blades. Provisions were, of course, made for his physical well being. The day's proceeds were donated to the Winter Relief Organization."

When the Second World War broke out, Bernhard Woldenga was in command of the I. *Gruppe* of JG 1. In mid-October 1940 he became *Kommodore* of JG 27 and in November of the same year of JG 77. Under his command, the latter unit achieved great success during the campaign in the Balkans and over

Crete, especially in low-level attacks. On 5 July 1941, *Major* Woldenga was awarded the Knight's Cross.

Another of the *Jagdgruppe's* pilots at Jesau was the then *Oberleutnant* Wilhelm Balthasar. He had also served in Spain, where he achieved seven confirmed victories. Balthasar succeeded in shooting down four Republican bombers in a single sortie on 7 February 1938.

When the Second World War began, Balthasar was a *Hauptmann* and *Staffelkapitän* in JG 27. The start of the Western Campaign in May 1940 marked the beginning of his most successful period. On the second day of the campaign, the 11th of May, he scored four victories, and more followed quickly. Balthasar shot down five enemy aircraft on 5 June 1940 and four more the next day. By the 13th of June his total stood at 23, making him the most successful fighter pilot of the campaign in France. On 14 June 1940 he became the second fighter pilot after Werner Mölders to receive the Knight's Cross.

Balthasar was named *Kommandeur* of the III. *Gruppe* of JG 3 prior to the start of the Battle of Britain. On 4 September 1940 he was wounded in both legs during an air battle over England but returned to action just fourteen days later. In February 1941 Balthasar took over JG 2 "Richthofen" as *Kommandeur*. By 27 June 1941 he raised his victory total to forty during operations over England and the Channel. In recognition, on 2 June 1941 Wilhelm Balthasar became the seventeenth member of the German Armed Services to receive the Oak Leaves.

On 3 July 1941, one day after receiving the Oak Leaves, took off on a maintenance test flight in a recently delivered Bf 109 F-4. As he was flying in the circuit, several RAF Spitfires suddenly appeared. Balthasar's aircraft carried no ammunition and he began taking evasive action. In the process he apparently overstressed his machine. The wings sheared off and the Messerschmitt crashed to the ground, killing Balthasar. The victor in a total of forty-seven air combats died because of a design error, one which had already claimed the lives of several pilots since the introduction of the new Me 109.

Back to the *Jagdgruppe* Jesau. The mood at the beginning of 1939 was set by another political event, the occupation of the Memel District.

Memelland was the name given to part of East Prussia situated east of the Memel River. The area was taken from Germany after the First World War and in 1920 was placed under French administration. Then in 1923 it was annexed by Lithuania.

The incorporation of the Sudetenland into the German Reich in October 1938 was followed by the destruction of what was left of the Czechoslovakian state. Slovakia became an independent nation, and the remaining Czech territories were incorporated into the Reich as the Reich Protectorate of Bohemia and Moravia.

And so the Memelland remained as one of Hitler's last demands resulting from the revision of the Versailles Treaty. Lithuania wanted to avoid a fate similar to the one suffered by Czechoslovakia. On 22 March 1939, one week after the German entry into Prague, Lithuania voluntarily returned the area to Germany.

The German occupation of the Memel District took place one day later. A fleet unit led by the pocket battleship "Deutschland" sailed into Memel. Hitler himself was on board and he personally took part into the German entry into the city. In addition to three army battalions, units of the Luftwaffe, including the *Jagdgruppe* Jesau, also took part.

The unit's aircraft landed at an airfield near the city of Memel. Their flight over the city was essentially for display purposes. The fighter pilots, among them Günther Scholz, did not stay long. After visiting the city they soon returned to East Prussia.

On 1 May 1939 Hitler created the Commemorative Medal of the Return of the Memel District. It was to be awarded to persons who had made a special contribution to the reunification of the Memel District with the German Reich. This included all those members of the army, the air force and the navy who had taken part in the occupation. The medal was awarded a total of 31,322 times. Günther Scholz received it in December 1939, at the same time as the Commemorative Medal of 1 October 1938, struck by Hitler on 18 October 1938 to mark the occupation of the Sudetenland.

Before he was awarded these two medals, Günther Scholz had received decorations for his service in Spain.

The Battle of the Ebro was raging when he left the country. The fighting dragged on until late autumn 1938. Soon afterwards, Franco launched an offensive in Catalonia, which concluded with the occupation of Barcelona on 26 January 1939. The Spanish Civil War had entered its final phase.

The Nationalists launched their final offensive on 16 March 1939. The Republican front collapsed. Madrid was taken and on 29 March the fighting stopped. There were weeklong celebrations and parades throughout the land. On 22 May Franco personally said goodbye to the "Legion Condor" on the occasion of its departure for Germany. The last legionnaires arrived in Hamburg aboard five ships of the Strength Through Joy organization on 31 May.

A great victory parade was scheduled for 6 June 1939. Thousands of men who had served in Spain were summoned to Berlin. Günther Scholz was again forced to interrupt his duties in East Prussia. Everyone who took part remembered the parade.

"It was an insanely hot day. We were wearing our Spanish uniforms with collars and ties. Many of us no longer had these and there was some hasty improvisation.

We were supposed to parade-march past a podium that had been set up for Hitler on the Unter den Linden. But first there was an interminable wait.

The German side lad lost more than 300 killed in Spain. A large plaque was made for each of the fallen, bearing the man's name. Soldiers, each with a plaque in his hands, formed up for the parade and the speeches.

All this time we waited near the Spree, where the trees offered some shade. Several of us keeled over from the long wait in the heat. More passed out in the square in front of the museum during the speeches. After we formed up, Hitler gave his speech. He was followed by Göring, and the Legion's commanders also said a few words. For us it was terrible, no wonder that some couldn't bear up. Only afterwards did the parade take place.

We also received our decorations that day. I was awarded the Spanish Cross in Gold with Swords and two Spanish decorations. One of them was the Cruz de Guerra, which was roughly equivalent to our Iron Cross, First Class. The other was called Medalla de Campagna and could be compared to the Iron Cross, Second Class.

The young women of Berlin were, of course, very attracted to the veterans of Spain. The Cruz de Guerra was very colorful, it had very pretty colors, and it even made a good brooch. I personally saw a number of men giving their medals to some girl."

The Spanish Cross, the decoration for members of the "Legion Condor", was issued in two versions, with swords and without. Each had three grades: bronze, silver and gold. In recognition of his successful service as a close-support and fighter pilot, Günther Scholz was awarded the Spanish Cross in Gold with Swords. This grade of the decoration was awarded a total of 1,126 times.

Also created was the Spanish Cross in Gold with Diamonds. Twenty-eight members of the Legion were awarded this decoration for particularly outstanding service in Spain. Among them were Adolf Galland, Werner Mölders and Wilhelm Balthasar.

In addition to decorations and early promotion to *Oberleutnant*, Günther Scholz's voluntary service in Spain gave him another advantage over his fellow fighter pilots. He now had operational experience. Passing this experience on to new pilots was of great importance in the still-expanding Luftwaffe.

After having been renamed I./JG 1 on 1 April 1939, on 15 July the former *Jagdgruppe* Jesau became the I. *Gruppe* of *Jagdgeschwader* 21. Its home was Gutenfeld airfield near Königsberg in East Prussia. The newly-created *Geschwader* again consisted of just a single *Gruppe* and was commanded by

Major **Martin Mettig, a general staff officer. Günther Scholz was named a** ***Staffelkapitän*** **and took over the 1.** ***Staffel.*** **The other two** ***Staffelkapitäne*** **were** ***Oberleutnante*** **Leo Eggers and Georg Schneider.**

Dark clouds were again gathering in the political sky as the new ***Jagdgruppe*** **trained in East Prussia. The new** ***Staffeln*** **developed into close-knit units.**

Another member of Günther Scholz's 1./JG 21 was ***Leutnant*** **Heinz Lange, who would later win the Knight's Cross. Born on 2 October 1917, Lange joined the air force in 1937. He left** ***Jagdgeschwader*** **26 "Schlageter" to join the new I./JG 21 at Gutenfeld.**

5
The War Begins

On 1 September 1939 the European crisis became a war. Germany marched into Poland, and soon afterwards Great Britain and France declared war on Germany.

On that 1st of September, the German armies crossed the Polish frontier. I./JG 21 moved from Gutenfeld to a forward airfield at Arys-Rostken on East Prussia's eastern border near the Mazurian Lakes. That afternoon the ***Gruppe*** **took off on its first mission over Poland.**

"The German people were less than enthusiastic when the war broke out, as were we soldiers. Everyone has seen the pictures from the First World War with soldiers heading for the front wearing flowers. Nowhere was this the case. The civilian population was rather subdued.

Our first mission was providing escort for a formation of He 111s that was supposed to attack targets near Warsaw. Before takeoff, we had selected an area of airspace in which we would rendezvous with the bombers. A flare was selected as a recognition signal.

It was our first real combat operation, and everyone was extremely nervous. As we approached the bomber formation, they suddenly began shooting at us. They probably took us for Poles, though in fact no such mistake should have been made. At that time the Poles were still flying high-wing monoplanes as fighters.

All of this made our commander, *Major* Mettig, nervous too. We had to fire the recognition signal as quickly as possible. A flare pistol had been installed in his aircraft for this purpose. When he fired the pistol, a white flare would shoot out the bottom of his machine and then burst into several red flares.

As *Major* Mettig fired the pistol, he noticed that it hadn't been properly secured to the floor of the cockpit. The recoil jerked it from its mount, and the flare landed in the machine and whizzed about his feet. Seconds later the flare burst and Mettig became frightened. What should he do?

First he jettisoned his canopy. Several of the flare elements were sucked out by the air pressure, but two continued whizzing about between his legs. Mettig reached down, grabbed them, and threw them out of the cockpit. For him the war had already ceased to be fun. The flares produced tremendous heat, and he received severe burns on both legs and his right hand. He immediately turned back and, with difficulty, flew home using his left hand.

The rest of us were dismayed. We didn't learn exactly what had happened in the cockpit of our commander until after the mission was over. The bombers had by then realized their mistake and carried on toward the target in a relatively orderly fashion. Then, as we approached Warsaw, there was an engagement with enemy aircraft.

We had taken off on our mission relatively late in the day. It was already late afternoon and the sun was going down. It was also quite hazy. The brief engagement caused us to lose our orientation. As I said before, few of us had any combat experience. Our formation broke up. The bomber crews later told us that we had suddenly all disappeared. They were nevertheless able to complete their mission virtually undisturbed. Afterwards they flew on to Upper Silesia instead of returning to East Prussia.

I, too, suddenly found myself all alone. My first thought was, where am I? How will I get home? I had memorized the map prior to takeoff. I remembered that there was a river running almost straight north in the direction of the East Prussian border. I looked around, and down below I saw the river in the failing light. The water gleamed in the sunset. All I had to do was follow it.

I flew along the river at an altitude of about 2,000 meters. When I reached the border I dropped down low so that I could make out and identify the various towns. In this way I found my way back to our airfield. At first I was flying alone, but later, one by one, I was joined by other aircraft. They had found me by chance and were happy to have someone show them the way.

As we were still at full peacetime strength, all twelve aircraft of my *Staffel* had taken off on this mission. Only eight returned, however; the rest had disappeared. We received news of their whereabouts the next day. Two members of my *Staffel* had been unable to find the airfield but had landed in East Prussia. One of the two had run out of fuel and came down in a meadow near Königsberg. Of the other two, there was no news."

The first mission by I./JG 21 had literally gone to the dogs. *Oberleutnant* Günther Scholz's 1. *Staffel* got off relatively lightly. Of the twelve aircraft that had taken off, ten eventually returned. In the case of the 3. *Staffel*, just two pilots made it back, the *Staffelkapitän Oberleutnant* Georg Schneider and *Leutnant* Hans-Ekkehard Bob.

The two missing pilots of the 1. *Staffel* were *Leutnant* Friedrich Behrens and his wingman *Unteroffizier* Otto Wolz. Both had been forced to come down in Polish territory and became prisoners of war.

Behrends managed to escape while the fighting in Poland was still going on. He made his way east to the Soviets, who had also invaded Poland in mid-September 1939. With the aid of the German embassy in Moscow, he returned to the *Gruppe*. Wolz, who was in hospital in Cracow, was freed by the Soviets. Like Behrends, he returned to his unit by way of Moscow.

I./JG 21 also achieved successes during the first days of the war. Five members of the *Gruppe* scored their first victories during their first combat mission, including *Oberleutnant* Schneider and *Leutnant* Rödel.

Born on 24 October 1915, Gustav Rödel had also gained his first operational experience in Spain. After the Polish Campaign, Rödel was transferred to the *Stab* of JG 27 as technical officer. Then, on 1 September 1940, he became *Staffelkapitän* of the 4. *Staffel*. By the end of the year, Rödel increased his victory total to 14 confirmed over France, the Channel and Great Britain. In the spring of 1941 he and his *Staffel* took part in the fighting in the Balkans and in June began operating over North Africa. On 22 June 1941 *Oberleutnant* Rödel was awarded the Knight's Cross for shooting down twenty enemy aircraft.

On 20 May 1942, Rödel was named *Kommandeur* of JG 27's II. *Gruppe*. About one year later, on 22 May 1943, he assumed command of the *Geschwader*. After his 78th victory, on 20 June 1943 Rödel became the 255th recipient of the Knight's Cross with Oak Leaves. When the war ended, Gustav Rödel was an *Oberst* and commander of the 2. *Jagddivision*. He had achieved ninety-eight confirmed victories in a total of 980 combat missions, all against Allied opponents in the west. His victory total included twelve heavy bombers.

"For our *Gruppe*, the Polish Campaign went on after the disastrous first mission. We flew one or two missions each day, but contact with the Polish air force was rare, as their air defenses had quickly collapsed.

And so we flew a series of low-level close-support missions, always along the roads in search of Polish columns or troop concentrations. On one occasion my *Staffel* and I attacked a battery of motorized artillery. The clouds of dust produced by the trucks made it easy to spot from a great distance. The column met its end on that road.

I took part in one air battle during the Polish Campaign, however I was unable to achieve a victory."

The German advance into Poland gained ground rapidly. Large elements of the Polish Army were encircled in the first days of the campaign. As stated, the pilots of I./JG 21 flew several sorties per day.

On 17 September 1939 the first members of I./JG 21 were awarded the Iron Cross, Second Class, including the *Staffelkapitäne* Günther Scholz, Leo Eggers and Georg Schneider, plus pilots Hans-Ekkehard Bob, Gustav Rödel and Heinz Lange.

One day later, on 18 September 1939, the Polish Commander-in-Chief Marshall Rydz-Smigly and most of his army surrendered. The encircled Polish capital continued to offer determined resistance. Hitler had decided to go to the front and inspect his troops. He and his staff drove to the front before Warsaw. Various Luftwaffe units were assigned the task of providing air cover for the column, including Günther Scholz and his *Staffel*.

"On 22 September 1939 I received orders for my *Staffel* and I to fly cover for the *Führer's* column at a certain time that day. This was no big thing. I was told from where and when the column would depart. The aircraft of my unit were to accompany it and circle overhead constantly until Hitler would complete his tour.

In the morning we took off from Arys-Rostken. The column stopped at lunchtime and we landed at a nearby airfield. The place was called Wyszkow. Cars drove us to the column's resting place. There was a great tumult there, as everyone wanted to see Hitler. He and his escorting generals ate a simple lunch, after which the column drove on. Another *Staffel* took over the job of providing air cover."

On 23 August 1939, before the start of the Polish Campaign, Germany and the Soviet Union had concluded a non-aggression pact, which included a secret protocol. As a result of this agreement, on 17 September 1939 the Soviet Union joined the war against Poland and occupied the eastern portion of the country.

After a major effort by the Luftwaffe, Warsaw capitulated on 27 September 1939. I./JG 21 moved to the airfield at Bialystok. According to the terms of the German-Russian agreement, the future demarcation line ran through this city. From their side of the airfield, the members of I./JG 21 could hear the Russians singing on the other side. After just a few days, the German airmen left the airfield and handed it completely over to the Russians. I./JG 21 moved back to Jesau in East Prussia.

6
Air War in the West

The campaign against Poland ended in victory after only a few weeks. By contrast, the situation on the Western Front had remained quiet. Great Britain and France had declared war, but they had not yet crossed the German frontier. During the fighting in Poland and in the weeks that followed, action on the Western Front was limited to isolated exchanges of fire.

After returning to East Prussia, I./JG 21 remained at Jesau for just a few days. In mid-October the *Gruppe* moved to Plantlünne in the Emsland to defend the airspace over Germany's western border. The *Gruppe's* stay there was also a short one. On 9 November 1939 it moved to Hopsten and on 3 December to Krefeld.

I./JG 21's path led it to Münster-Handorf on 8 December 1939. During the period around the turn of the year, the *Gruppe* was reequipped with the Me 109 E. On 28 January 1940 the *Gruppe* moved south Mönchen-Gladbach in the Rhineland, where it was to remain until the invasion of Western Europe.

The transfer flight was made in terrible rainy weather. When the aircraft landed at Mönchen-Gladbach they sank to their axles in mud. These conditions kept the *Gruppe* grounded for several days.

There had still not been any serious fighting. In small formations, the German fighters flew defensive patrols in the airspace up to the French border. Now and then there were encounters with lone British or French reconnaissance machines. The German fighters were forbidden from overflying enemy territory.

On 1 February 1940 *Major* Martin Mettig left the *Gruppe* and was succeeded by *Hauptmann* Fritz Ultsch. The defensive patrols continued, and the *Staffelkapitäne* molded their units. New pilots were given additional training at the unit level. In March 1940 a young man was transferred to Günther Scholz's *Staffel* who would later become one of the Luftwaffe's leading fighter pilots. His name was *Leutnant* Max-Hellmuth Ostermann.

Born on 11 December 1917, Ostermann had joined the Luftwaffe as an officer candidate in late 1937 after completing school and had been promoted to *Leutnant* just before the outbreak of war. Assigned to the I. *Gruppe* of *Zerstörergeschwader* 1, he flew his first missions over Poland on the Me 110. Now Ostermann was joining a single-seat unit. In the spring of 1940 no one suspected that this young *Leutnant* would have such an impressive flying career, especially as he initially had some difficulty mastering the Me 109.

"Ostermann was quite short in stature. In his early days as a fighter pilot this caused him some problems. The Me 109 had a tendency to swing to the side on landing. The Messerschmitt's undercarriage was extremely narrow. If the propeller was subjected to a strong crosswind on landing, the machine very quickly veered to the side. In order to prevent this and keep the Messerschmitt on course, one had to brake to left or right. Landing in a strong crosswind was relatively difficult. Now and then green pilots cracked up, performing what we called a *Ringelpietz** (**Ringelpietz*: a game played by German children, in which they hold hands and dance in a circle. In Luftwaffe slang the word came to mean a ground loop). This meant that the aircraft swung and the rapid rotary motion caused the narrow undercarriage to shear off. The Me 109 ended up on a wing and the undercarriage was also usually damaged.

Ostermann made two or three such ground loops in his first weeks with our *Staffel*. Because of his stature, he simply had problems reaching the brake pedals or applying the necessary force. Exactly who came up with the idea, or whether it was Ostermann himself, I can no longer remember, but he subsequently fitted wooden blocks on his pedals. In this manner he was able to properly control his machine and prevent further crash-landings. One often reads that Ostermann had these wooden blocks installed in his cockpit so that, as a dogfighting specialist, he could fly even tighter turns in the air. This may well have helped him during combat, but the measure was mainly necessary so that he could land the Messerschmitt safely."

Soon after the end of the fighting in Poland, Hitler wanted to seize the initiative and attack the western powers. Many of the German generals were opposed to the idea, recalling the painful losses on the western front during the First World War. Between November 1939 and May 1940, the date for the attack in the west was postponed a dozen times for different reasons. To make matters worse, in January the plans for the German buildup fell into Allied hands.

The German offensive in the west began on 10 May 1940. A new attack plan had been developed which called for the main thrust to be made through Holland and Belgium into northern France. The heavily-fortified Maginot Line would literally be bypassed on the left.

I./JG 21 was attached to the VIII. *Fliegerkorps*. Operations intensified even before the attack. The pilots entered French airspace several times, but there were no serious encounters with enemy aircraft.

German troops achieved major successes on the first two days of the campaign, driving deep into Holland and Belgium. On 12 May 1940, I./JG 21

moved from Mönchen-Gladbach to Vogelsang. One day later *Oberleutnant* Günther Scholz scored his first victory in this new war. On 13 May 1940 he shot down a Curtiss* (*Hawk 75 A-1/4, an export version of the P-36 flown by the Armée de l'Air) in an engagement over Belgium, east of Löwen.

After flying its first missions from Vogelsang in Germany, beginning on 16 May I./JG 21 moved in rapid succession to a variety of forward airfields in Belgium and France. The Dutch Army surrendered to the Germans on 14 May.

The primary mission of the fighter pilots was escorting the Stuka and bomber units supporting the army. They also flew a number of *freie Jagd missions over enemy territory. (*Literally "free hunt". Fighter sweeps in which a fighter unit went looking for targets of opportunity.) On 20 May 1940 *Oberleutnant* Scholz scored his second victory, in the area west of Péronne. That same day young *Leutnant* Ostermann shot down his first enemy aircraft. In mid-May JG 21 entered northern France.**

"Among the places where we stopped during our march through France, I remember Cambrai especially well. There, during the First World War, my father had taken part in the first big tank battle in history as a flamethrower operator. Now I, his son, was passing over the same blood-soaked earth.

On 26 May 1940 my *Staffel* and I engaged enemy aircraft in this area. I suddenly saw an enemy machine heading for me, and we flew straight towards each other. When we got closer, my opponent snapped into a turn in an effort to get on my tail. I also applied full rudder and the dogfight was on. I rammed the throttle full forward in order to get around even more quickly. This enabled me to maintain speed as the turns became tighter. I also engaged my flaps in order to slow the machine somewhat at the moment I got behind him. I had practiced this maneuver a number of times.

We were at a height of about 2,000 meters, the sky was cloudy, but there was no solid cloud deck. After about the fourth turn I gradually got behind him. Then he made a mistake. Instead of trying to shake me off by diving, he pulled up. He was apparently trying to reach the clouds, but in doing so he put himself right in my sights. I pressed the firing buttons and my bullets found the mark. As I watched he entered the clouds, then there was a bright explosion.

Finding myself alone, I set course for home. Then, off to the side, I noticed another French aircraft. I turned towards it. He apparently hadn't spotted me. I used the element of surprise to position myself on his tail and score my second victory for that day. There was no dogfight.

Army troops later confirmed both of my victories."

Günther Scholz's two victories on that 26 May 1940 raised his total during the Western Campaign to four. *Leutnant* Ostermann scored his second victory. One day earlier, on 25 May 1940, *Oberleutnant* Scholz had been awarded the Iron Cross, First Class.

Despite the doubts of the generals, the German attack in the west produced an unprecedented victory. Belgium surrendered a few days after Holland. The British Expeditionary Corps and part of the French Army were driven back to the Channel and encircled in the Dunkirk area. There the German advance halted, enabling the British to evacuate approximately 340,000 Allied troops to England. The Luftwaffe alone operated against the evacuation, attacking enemy shipping round the clock. Once again, I./JG 21 flew escort for the German bomber units

The second phase, the actual Battle of France, began at the beginning of June 1940. During the fighting, I./JG 21 moved to a variety of airfields, ending up in the Paris area. On 21 June 1940 the fighting in the west ended when France signed a ceasefire agreement.

One day after the defeat of France, I./JG 21 returned to Mönchen-Gladbach, then on 23 June 1940 it moved to Holland.

"My 1. *Staffel* and I went to Bergen am See. Our task was to defend Dutch airspace against incursions by the British. The time was also used to bring the *Gruppe* up to strength in men and machines. The weeks that followed were a quiet, pleasant time. While we flew regular fighter sweeps, at first there was no trace of the big war.

Once in a while we flew out over the sea, but not as far as England. Now and then the British sent several Blenheims over the mainland, mainly on reconnaissance. These incursions sometimes resulted in combat. *Oberleutnant* Georg Schneider, *Staffelkapitän* of the 3. *Staffel*, was lost in one such action on 27 June 1940.

Schneider and his *Staffel* were based at nearby Soesterberg. On the 27th three Blenheim bombers appeared over the 3. *Staffel's* dispersal. *Oberleutnant* Schneider led a *Schwarm** into the air. (**Schwarm*: flight of four aircraft, the standard tactical formation of the German fighter arm.) He managed to shoot down one of the Blenheims, however its dorsal gunner scored hits first. Schneider probably got too close, and pieces of the exploding machine struck his aircraft. These two reasons caused Schneider to lose control of his Messerschmitt. His altitude was not great, as he had attacked the Blenheims immediately after scrambling from the field. He was unable to regain control of his aircraft – he may also have been wounded – and crashed into the ground.

We three *Staffelkapitäne* of I./JG 21 – Eggers, Schneider and I – had been close friends. Now one was gone."

***Oberleutnant* Georg Schneider had scored two victories over Poland and added four more over France. The British Blenheim he shot down on 27 June 1940 was his seventh and last victory.**

Georg Schneider's successor as *Staffelkapitän* of the 3. *Staffel* was *Oberleutnant* Richard Hausmann. He had been transferred to I./JG 21 at the end of November 1939 and had flown in the 2. *Staffel.*

There had been another personnel change on 8 June 1940. *Leutnant* Heinz Lange had left the 1. *Staffel* and been transferred to the *Stab* of JG 54 as adjutant. He had recorded his one and only victory on 30 September 1940, when he shot down a Blenheim.

In August 1940 Heinz Lange was promoted to *Oberleutnant* and at the end of the month he returned to III./JG 54 and flew in the 8. *Staffel.* It was not until 30 June 1941, in Russia, that he recorded his second victory. By 23 September 1941 he increased his victory total to seven. Soon afterwards he was named *Staffelkapitän* of 1./JG 54 and by 20 September 1942 he added another thirteen victories.

On 6 November 1942 Lange moved to JG 51, where he served as commander of the 3. *Staffel*, and in February 1943 he was promoted to *Hauptmann.* On 16 October 1940 he achieved his fiftieth victory. At the beginning of January 1944 he returned to JG 54, taking over the I. *Gruppe* as acting commander. On 9 May 1944 Lange was named *Gruppenkommandeur* of IV./JG 51. Whilst serving in that position, he was awarded the Knight's Cross on 18 November 1944. He had scored his seventieth and last victory on 15 October 1944. Following promotion to *Major* on 1 January 1945, at the beginning of April Lange became the last *Kommodore* of JG 54. Leading the *Geschwader*, he flew his final combat mission over Berlin on 29 April 1945.

Back to the summer of 1940. On 15 July 1940 I./JG 21 was renamed III./JG 54. The 1., 2. and 3. *Staffel* of I./JG 21 became the 7., 8. and 9. *Staffel* of JG 54. Commanding the *Geschwader* was *Major* Mettig, who had been in charge of the *Geschwader* since leaving I./JG 21. The renaming of I./JG 21 brought JG 54's strength up to three *Jagdgruppen.*

After the defeat of France, Great Britain was Germany's sole remaining opponent. The bulk of the British Expeditionary Corps had avoided destruction and escaped to England. Hitler wanted to spare the English enemy. When the war on the continent ended, he sent a peace offer to London. The overture was ignored, and Britain would carry on the war without France.

At the same time as it was proposing a peace settlement, Germany was also making plans for an invasion of Great Britain. Even while the campaign against France was still under way, the German air force had flown attacks against British merchant shipping and ports on the English Channel. The bulk of its units had still been tied down in France, however. Now the Luftwaffe was to assume the main burden of the war against Great Britain. Before the navy could land units of the army on the British Isles, the air force first had to achieve air superiority over the Channel and the south of England. This part of the Second World War would later go down in history as the "Battle of Britain".

The first phase of the campaign took place in the summer and lasted until 24 July 1940. The Luftwaffe assembled ten fighter and three *Zerstörer** wings on the Channel plus bomber, dive-bomber and reconnaissance units. (**Zerstörer*: Literally "destroyer", referred to a class of long-range heavy fighter of which the Bf 110 was the first example.)

After the German buildup on the Channel was completed, the second phase of the air battle began. It lasted from 24 July until 8 August 1940 and was played out mainly over the Channel. The German fighter units fought fierce battles against their British counterparts.

JG 54 flew its first missions from its bases in Holland, but beginning on 6 August it moved to well-concealed airfields in the Calais area. The III. *Gruppe* was based at Guines.

The German fighter pilots flew constantly, usually three or four missions per day. The physical and psychological strain was enormous and both sides suffered heavily in the fighter-versus-fighter duels. Gradually the air battle shifted from the Channel to the south of England. As both sides sought to gain an altitude advantage over the enemy, the battles were fought at ever greater altitudes.

The strategic objectives set by the Luftwaffe command could not be achieved. It had been hoped that the fighter-versus-fighter duels would result in the destruction of RAF Fighter Command at relatively little cost to the Luftwaffe. Before this was achieved, however, the British command pulled its fighter units back, abandoning its coastal airfields and falling back to airfields on a line in front of London.

The German side was forced to change its tactics. This resulted in the third phase of the campaign, which was to last from 8 August until 7 September 1940. The fighter arm had failed to achieve air superiority over the south of England on its own. Now the bombers were to carry out raids on British airfields and centers where the manufacture of aircraft and power

plants was carried out. Instead of free-ranging fighter sweeps, the German fighters were now tied to the bombers.

The British fighters rejoined the battle, intercepting the bomber formations and producing huge air battles. Günther Scholz scored three victories during this phase of the campaign. On 25 August 1940 he shot down his first Spitfire. This was followed by a Hurricane on 28 August and another Spitfire on 2 September. All three enemy machines were shot down over the south of England.

"Flying escort missions was tiresome work. The bomber formations flew very slowly and the fighters had to throttle back to stay with them. In doing so, we surrendered our advantage over the British fighters.

The first missions we flew in formation with the bombers. One *Staffel* flew beneath the formation, one above and the other to the side. This was later abandoned on account of our superior speed and we switched to circling the bombers. We flew in various formations and at different altitudes, but we always had to stay with the bombers.

We met the English fighters almost as soon as we crossed the Channel. They usually attacked from above and were literally waiting for us. If it was a sunny day, we could se the sun glinting off their canopies and wings from far away. They came down fast, right through the throng of German fighters, tried to close with a bomber or even shoot it down, then they broke away. That was their tactic. They rarely approached our formation from the side or below, for then the advantage would be with us.

If the Spitfires came down from above at high speed, they were too fast to catch. To be sure we kept a constant lookout above in an effort to see them in time, but suddenly they were among us. Of course some of them were shot down, but by attacking in this manner they hit many of our bombers.

We were under orders to always stay with the bombers. We could only engage the enemy if it was to prevent an English fighter from shooting down one of our bombers. But that was just in theory. In practice, combats broke out everywhere as soon as the swarms of Hurricanes or Spitfires fell from the heavens.

All of this made it very difficult for the unit leaders to command properly in the air. As soon as a few fighters broke away to engage the English, a general dogfight broke out. The bombers then complained to the *Geschwader* or the *Jagdfliegerführer** that the fighters had disappeared at the start of the battle. (**Jagdfliegerführer*: abbreviated *Jafü*, literally "fighter leader". The commander of fighter units, early in the war within an air fleet, later also within specific geographical areas. The *Jafü* 2 was the commander of fighter units within *Luftflotte* 2, for example. In May 1944

Scholz became *Jagdfliegerführer* Norwegen, which was attached to *Luftflotte* 5.) They felt alone and abandoned and were relieved to make it home in one piece.

The bomber formations usually avoided flying the same route to and from the target. If, for example, they attacked airfields near London, instead of flying straight back across the Channel they would follow the coast of southern England for some distance in the direction of Cherbourg in Normandy. The bombers thus flew a greater distance over water and the English fighters did not follow, in part because they lacked the fuel.

No airman likes flying over water. The longer one has to fly over water, the faster one's spirits sink. If one's machine was hit and one had to bale out, it meant coming down in the water. This was a dangerous thing, especially in the far north. Hypothermia could develop quickly, even in summer. Every pilot wore a life vest, and many even had an inflatable life raft. I never had one during my time on the Channel. Later, when we were flying over the Arctic Ocean, the life raft was attached to our parachutes.

The air-sea rescue service was the last hope for a missing or shot-down pilot. But even these seaplanes, which were marked with large red crosses, were attacked by the English. I never witnessed this personally, but it happened a number of times.

We flew across the Channel with the bombers at relatively high altitude, 4,000 to 5,000 meters. If there were air battles, and there usually were, we usually dropped to the lower altitudes. For the return flight we climbed back up to 2,000 to 3,000 meters. If there was more fighting near the Channel and one's machine was hit, it was still possible to glide to the French coast. The coast there was sandy and broad, and many used it for belly landings. If there was no other choice, one could ditch in the Channel or, in the worst case, bale out over England.

We flew at least three or four sorties per day, sometimes even five. It was a war of nerves, which some could not endure in the long run. One such man was our *Staffelkapitän* Eggers. He became extremely nervous and didn't want to fly anymore. Every time one taxied out for takeoff, one knew that it might be for the last time. For Eggers the nervous strain simply became too much. Flown out, we called it. He was relieved and replaced. For all those who endured, the missions went on."

By the time he was relieved as *Kapitän* of the 8. *Staffel*, *Oberleutnant* Leo Eggers had shot down four enemy aircraft – one over Poland, two during the French campaign and one while the unit was stationed in Holland. Later, when JG 54 established its *Ergänzungsstaffel, Eggers became its first commander. (**Ergänzungsstaffel*: *Staffel*-size unit responsible for training replacement**

pilots before they were assigned to an operational unit.) In the spring the *Staffel* was expanded into an *Ergänzungsgruppe and *Hauptmann* Eggers became *Kommandeur.* (**Ergänzungsgruppe*: *Gruppe*-size unit responsible for training replacement pilots before they were assigned to an operational unit.) When the *Ergänzungsgruppe* was disbanded at the beginning of 1942, Eggers was assigned to *Jagdfliegerschule* 2* at Zerbst as commanding officer. (**Jagdfliegerschule*: an advanced flying school where students were taught to fly fighter aircraft.) Leo Eggers was killed in action in 1943 while serving with JG 3 in the east.**

Eggers' successor as commander of 8./JG 54 was *Oberleutnant* Richard Hausmann, who handed command of the 9. *Staffel* over to *Oberleutnant* Hans-Ekkehard Bob.

There had been a change in the *Geschwader* command of JG 54 on 25 August 1940, when *Major* Martin Mettig handed the unit over to *Major* Hannes Trautloft.

The third phase of the air battle had also failed to produce the desired results for the German side. The bombing raids against British airfields had been largely ineffective. For one thing, hitting a British fighter on the ground was a matter of chance, for these usually took to the air to intercept the approaching formation, and the quantity of bombs dropped was insufficient to cause large-scale destruction. Usually the British were able to make their airfields serviceable again during the night.

The fourth phase of the Battle of Britain began on 7 September 1940. German raids were no longer limited to British airfields and aircraft factories, instead they were expanded to include other industrial targets. The German aerial offensive was also expanded territorially, and the British capital became the main target of the German incursions.

"On 5 December 1940 *Hauptmann* Ultsch, our *Gruppenkommandeur*, was shot down during a mission over England. As I was the senior *Staffelkapitän*, I took over command of the *Gruppe* for a time. With this came additional responsibilities.

We received our mission orders from the *Jagdfliegerführer*, also called the *Jafü*. Either these were sent through the *Geschwaderstab** or the *Gruppenkommandeur* received his instructions directly from the *Jafü*. (**Geschwaderstab*: a *Geschwader* headquarters). One was advised that we had to fly escort for bombers the next day, and details were provided as to which unit was involved and the timing and location of the rendezvous. Sometimes the staff passed this information on to us from the *Jafü*, but usually we contacted the bomber unit by telephone ourselves and worked out the details, in order to avoid mix-ups or disagreements.

Before a mission, the *Gruppenkommandeur* called his *Staffelkapitäne* together to discuss everything one more time, and sometimes the pilots also took part. At these briefings all of the participants were given the details of the coming mission. If it was an escort mission, then it was laid down in advance exactly where each *Staffel* was to take its place and who was to fly *freie Jagd* around the formation. The chosen target and the agreed-upon rendezvous point with the bombers were discussed again and any remaining questions were answered. Then we headed out.

If one was flying *freie Jagd*, one was merely assigned a specific block of airspace in which to do so. Command of the unit was then left completely to the *Kommandeur**. (**Kommandeur*: the commanding officer of a *Gruppe*). If large-scale air battles involving a considerable number of aircraft developed, a commander's ability to effectively lead his unit diminished very rapidly.

Radio traffic turned into a terrific roar. Everyone was nervous and excited, and everyone shouted out whatever came into his mind. It was a terrific din. One had to watch one's tail constantly to make sure there was no one there. At the same time, one also had to watch for targets. If one did get behind an enemy machine, it was of course no easy thing to shoot it down. It was a constant up and down, back and forth. Maintaining situational awareness was not easy.

The *Gruppenkommandeur* had his own *Schwarm*. Four aircraft made up a *Schwarm*, and three *Schwärme* formed a *Staffel*. The *Gruppenschwarm* consisted of the *Gruppenkommandeur*, the adjutant, the technical officer and a non-commissioned officer, usually a *Feldwebel*. Before a mission started, the *Kommandeur* decided with which *Staffel* he wanted to fly. With his *Schwarm* he led the *Staffel*, and the others formed up on him.

We took off from the airfield in sequence and then began a climb to the assigned altitude. This interval was also used to form up and bring the formation together. To facilitate this, the *Gruppenkommandeur*, who was usually the first to take off, did not immediately apply full power. When he saw that everyone was in position on the left and right, he led the unit in formation to the rendezvous point. Sometimes the bombers were already there, sometimes they were late. That annoyed us, for it meant that we had to circle in the air. The longer we had to wait, the more fuel we consumed, and this of course affected the amount of time left for the actual mission. We tried to circle as close to the French coast as possible. The English fighters appeared as soon as we neared the English coast, their radar stations having informed them of our approach.

Once the bomber unit had arrived and the escorting *Staffeln* had taken up their positions, they headed out together across the Channel. If there were air battles, every pilot was left more or less on his own. After about 1 1/2 hours flying time at the latest, the red warning lights began coming on in the cockpits, the sign that fuel was running low. By this point at the latest, one had to begin thinking about the flight home. Even if one was still in formation, there was no choice but to turn around and fly back over the Channel. After all, it benefited no one if one was forced to come down in the British Isles with an empty fuel tank.

If one headed for home alone, low on fuel, there was always the danger that one might be attacked by British fighters lurking near the French coast. If this happened, one either had to land on the beach with one's last drops of fuel or ditch in the Channel, otherwise one would be shot down. One therefore had to try one's best to get home safely and, if possible, avoid being drawn into a dogfight.

We continued flying several missions each day. Sometimes a rest day was scheduled, but this was very rare. Most took advantage of these occasions to rest and catch up on sleep. Some took their cars and went on small outings, to Lille for example.

One incident stands out in my memory from the time of our flights to London. Now and again we had to take part in fierce air battles. A tremendous dogfight was in progress. Unnoticed by me, a Spitfire had positioned itself behind me. I received a warning call just in the nick of time: "Attention Number One, Indians behind you!" Indians was our code word for British fighters. The British, on the other hand, called us bandits. I found our term a little more refined.

As soon as I heard the warning, I turned around and saw a Spitfire quite close behind me and shooting. I saw the red-yellow flashes of its machine-guns. The Spitfire had four of them, two in each wing. At that time I was flying a Messerschmitt with steel back armor in the cockpit. It was attached to the rear part of the canopy and extended from the hips to above the head. As far as I can remember, our entire *Gruppe* was so equipped. Later I didn't see this back armor again.

The Englishman's aim was good. Not only did I see the muzzle flashes, but I also heard bullets striking behind me. Without the armor the battle would have been over, but as it was the bullets merely left three dents in my back armor.

We were at a height of about 4,000 meters. Instinctively, I made a Split-S and dove about 3,000 meters. All of this happened in fractions of seconds. I was lucky: the Englishman didn't follow me. I suspect that it was a young and not so experienced pilot, otherwise he would have pursued me. Or perhaps he was certain that he had shot me down. In his eyes, after all, his bullets had found their mark. He had every reason to believe that they might possibly have killed me, and he could have interpreted the dive as a machine spinning towards the ground out of control.

Whatever the case, it was a tremendous piece of luck for me. After I pulled the Messerschmitt out of its dive, I checked over the machine for damage. The radio was no longer working. It was located aft in the fuselage and there couldn't have been much left of it from the Spitfire's bullets. My cockpit had thus become quiet.

I heard nothing more of all the shouting during the air battle. On the other hand, I was now out of contact with my people. I had to get back to them.

There wasn't much more I could do. The incident had taken place southeast of London. The fighting was surely still in progress. I flew in the direction of home. Near the Channel I noticed that the coolant temperature was rising, apparently the cooling system had been hit too. I throttled back the engine, hoping there were no more Spitfires or Hurricanes nearby. But I made it across the Channel unmolested and was able to land safely at Guines.

That was the second incident that I had survived with a great deal of luck. *Leutnant* Behrens' warning and my back armor had saved my life. That it happened at all was my fault alone. My mistake had been that I was too busy scanning the airspace in front of me for opportunities of perhaps finding a victim myself. In doing so, I had failed to look behind for several minutes."

Some indication of the ferocity and cost of these air battles can be derived from the fact that on 18 September 1940, JG 54 could put just eighteen serviceable Me 109s into the air. Günther Scholz was able to shoot down a Spitfire on 28 September. It was his fourth victory during the Battle of Britain and his eighth overall.

The German air force command overestimated its own claims of success. Airfields that were attacked were classified as destroyed and estimates of Fighter Command losses were far too high. This led to a discrepancy between the Luftwaffe command's assessment of the situation and the actual conditions on the Channel.

"Once we were visited by *Generaloberst* Erhard Milch, a friend of Göring. We had to form up on the airfield and listen as Milch gave a vainglorious speech. He praised us for our high victory total and urged us to continue our successful ways, which would soon lead to the defeat of England's air force. The Luftwaffe command was quite confident of this; one only had to check the high victory figures.

Why is he talking such nonsense, I thought to myself? When we flew across the Channel they came down on us from above like the warm rain. And not just in ones and twos, but in large numbers. There were always heated air battles. If the *Generaloberst* would only climb into one of our aircraft and fly just one mission over England, he would see for himself how things really are. Fat chance of that!

The Luftwaffe command may well have compiled its statistics and calculations, only they didn't seem to add up, or they forgot to factor in that the English were receiving supplies of new machines. In any case the reality looked much different than what Milch tried to portray to us in his speech.

Looking back today, I am no longer certain that the victory claims we made back then were 100% accurate. After each victory one had to write a report using a prepared form. One had to enter the required information, for example the location and time of the victory, what type of aircraft it was, and at what altitude the combat had taken place, whether one observed an explosion or crash, etc. Then one needed a witness, who had to confirm the information.

A typical air battle involved 50 to 100 aircraft, all twisting and turning. Suddenly someone shouted into the radio: "I've shot one down!" If the *Rotte** was still together, then the wingman could confirm the victory, but in big battles sometimes even the *Rotte* became split up. (**Rotte*: a flight of two aircraft, element leader and wingman). How to obtain a confirmation then? I have no difficulty imagining that this could be part of the reason why our command assumed that the English were on the verge of defeat. Their calculations contained a number of victories which in fact were not victories.

I do not want to say that false claims were made, absolutely not. But I think back to my own experience with the Spitfire on my tail. Perhaps the Englishman claimed me as a kill too. However, I landed again uninjured, at least physically. The aircraft was repaired.

We spent most of our time flying over the Channel or English territory. For an aircraft that came down in the Channel there could be no subsequent confirmation by ground troops, as had been the case, for example, when I scored my double during the French Campaign."

The Luftwaffe suffered heavy losses in the fourth phase of the Battle of Britain. The fighters were unable to protect the bombers on their flights to metropolitan London. Instead of changing tactics back to the concept of concentrating solely on the English fighters and releasing the German fighters from their escort duties, the Luftwaffe command came up with an entirely different idea.

If the fighters were unable to protect the bombers, then they would carry the bombs to England themselves. The idea of the *Jabo* or fighter-bomber was born. II./LG 2 was selected to test the concept. Beginning on 20 September 1940, each day about thirty *Jabos* from the unit attacked targets in the south of England and the London area. These early missions caught the English by surprise, and so on the German side it was decided to assign *Jabo* missions to additional *Geschwader*.

III./JG 54 received its first three *Jabos* on 20 September 1940. They were Me 109s converted to carry bombs. Escorted by regular fighters, a small number of pilots were supposed to drop 250-kg bombs from these machines. The *Gruppe* did not fly its first such mission until 5 October, however.

This experimental mission was flown by *Oberleutnant* Scholz, *Oberleutnant* Bob, *Oberleutnant* Lange and *Leutnant* Wübke. The four aircraft took off from Guines in the late afternoon and flew to Calais-Marck, where II./LG 2 was based, to have the bombs fitted. From there they took off again at 17:52 hours. Their target was English coastal positions near Dungeness. The fighter-bombers attacked in a shallow dive and achieved three hits in the target area. All four aircraft landed back at Guines at 18:25. The pilots were very much less than enthusiastic about the mission.

The 8. and 9. *Staffel* of III./JG 54 flew two more *Jabo* missions by 12 October 1940. On that day all of the fighter-bombers were handed over to the 9. *Staffel*, which conducted additional sorties until 20 October, when bad weather halted operations.

"We were not at all enthusiastic about this *Jabo* idea. A 250-kg bomb is a rather heavy thing for a fighter aircraft. Just taking off with it was not simple. The extra weight lengthened the takeoff roll considerably. That was alright at the Guines airfield, which was large enough. At other airfields this was not the case.

One also had to avoid air combat. With a bomb under its belly the machine was completely incapable of maneuvering. There was nothing else to do but get rid of the monster as quickly as possible.

The aiming process was complicated too. One was supposed to approach the target at a certain altitude at a certain speed. As soon as the target began disappearing beneath the wing, one was supposed to drop the bomb.

The first such missions at the end of September 1940 caused the English much consternation. We learned this from monitoring their radio traffic. They had seen several bombs land, but no bombers had been sighted. It didn't take the English very long to figure out what was going on. The element of surprise was gone, and with it the whole point of the fighter-bomber missions. In reality, the bomb-carrying Messerschmitt made no sense and achieved nothing.

One of our missions, on 8 October 1940, was aimed at the London Docks, the big shipyards on the Thames. Our target was the docks, not the city.

We reached the target area without being intercepted. As we approached the London Docks I searched for my target. As planned, I was flying at a specific speed at a specific altitude. When my selected target began disappearing beneath my wing, I released the bomb. I tried to follow its path, curious to see where it would land. Definitely not where I had been aiming. I couldn't see anything, however. I had absolutely no idea where my bomb was heading. The London Docks were a bigger target than isolated coastal positions. Some even achieved the desired hit."

The fourth phase of the Battle of Britain ended on 20 October 1940. Bad weather was the final reason that led the Luftwaffe command to halt the costly daylight raids against London. That same day the Luftwaffe began its night bombing campaign. This marked the beginning of the final phase of the battle, in which the fighter units played no part.

The Luftwaffe's operational strength had fallen by about twenty-five percent since the beginning of August 1940. The German side called off the battle without having achieved the desired results, but it could scarcely be called a defeat. For England, however, it was a prestigious victory. The English fighters had fought off the Luftwaffe.

Günther Scholz scored four victories over England, raising his total to eight. Max-Hellmuth Ostermann had scored six victories, the last southeast of London on 20 October 1940, the final day of operations over England. Ostermann's victory total now matched that of his *Staffelkapitän*.

On 28 September 1940, the day of his eighth victory, *Oberleutnant* Günther Scholz was awarded the Honor Goblet for his success in the air war. This coveted award had been created by Hermann Göring, Commander-in-Chief of the Luftwaffe, on 27 February 1940. It was first awarded at the beginning of July 1940.

Günther Scholz was one of the first recipients of the Honor Goblet. Other members of JG 54 were similarly honored on 28 September, including *Hauptmann* Dietrich Hrabak, *Oberleutnant* Hans-Ekkehard Bob, *Oberleutnant* Hans Philipp and *Oberfeldwebel* Max Stotz.

On 21 October 1940, *Hauptmann* Dietrich Hrabak, *Kommandeur* of the II. *Gruppe*, became the first member of JG 54 to be awarded the Knight's Cross of the Iron Cross. His victory total on that day stood at sixteen. Just one day later, on 22 October 1940, *Oberleutnant* Hans Philipp was also awarded the Knight's Cross. The *Staffelkapitän* of 4./JG 54 had scored his twentieth victory on 20 October 1940.

7
Interludes

After the Luftwaffe command called off the aerial offensive against England and switched to night bombing, the *Jagdgeschwader* on the Channel front were moved one *Gruppe* at a time back to bases in the rear to rest and reequip.

On 21 October 1940, III./JG 54 received orders to move to Holland. Once again, the *Gruppe* was to be used in the air defense role. Late that same afternoon, *Oberleutnant* Scholz took off with the first pilots for Schipol. In Holland III./JG 54 received a new commanding officer. *Hauptmann* Arnold Lignitz assumed command on 4 November 1940. He had previously served as a *Staffelkapitän* in JG 51 and had nineteen victories to his credit, which had earned him the Knight's Cross on 5 November.

Günther Scholz had led the *Gruppe* in an acting capacity for about one and a half months and had been through some tough battles with it. On 28 October 1940 he returned to the head of his 7. *Staffel.*

"We were based at Utrecht at first and then at Schipol near Amsterdam. It was a very quiet time and the rest did us all good and was long overdue. The proximity of the Dutch capital city also gave us the opportunity to amuse ourselves and turn our thoughts to other things now and again.

This period ended on 4 December 1940 and these followed a period of winter quiet at Dortmund and Delmenhorst. The aircraft were overhauled and the *Staffel* brought back up to authorized strength. We were also able to take leave, and of course many took advantage of the opportunity.

In mid-January 1941 we returned to France, this time to the Le Mans area. My *Staffel* and I went to Cherbourg, from where we resumed operations against England, principally against the southern port cities of Plymouth and Southampton.

These flights were a very unhappy affair, as they covered longer stretches of water than the hop across the Channel from Guines. At that time the English did not venture as far as Cherbourg, so at least the air situation over Normandy was very quiet.

Our role was once again to escort the bombers, whose mission was to attack British warships in their ports. The bombers took off from the Orleans area or Le Mans. We rendezvoused with them over the Isle of Wight.

These missions were very different from those during the so-called Battle of Britain. Back then we had an excellent view of the Channel from our altitude. From 5,000 meters over the French Coast one could see the British Isles and vice versa. Now we took off from Cherbourg, climbed to an altitude of 6,000 to 7,000 meters and initially flew out over the Channel for a quarter of an hour. Only then did the coast of England slowly come into view. We first made out the Isle of Wight and soon afterwards the large cities of Plymouth or Southampton became visible.

There was relatively little combat at that time. By the time we reached the Isle of Wight we had already used up quite a lot of fuel. If we were lucky, we rendezvoused with the bombers on time. Usually, however, this was not the case and we had to go looking or wait for them. We didn't have a lot of time remaining, and we always had to take our return flight into consideration. This we usually did with engine throttled back and the warning lamp on, the sign that our fuel was slowly but surely running out.

These missions over long stretches of water were extremely unpleasant. One listened to the sound of the motor with an ever more critical ear. If it began to vibrate a little or made a noise that didn't sound normal, then the doubts began. Hopefully it wouldn't quit. Will I make it to the coast? Each minute seemed to last an eternity."

In addition to the missions over England, *Major* Trautloft, the *Kommodore* of JG 54, placed special emphasis on improving flight training and bolstering the team spirit within the unit. For example, none of those who were there will ever forget an evening spent together by the pilots of the two *Gruppen* based at Le Mans. On that occasion Trautloft used an air force dagger to "knight as fighter pilots" all of the new pilots recently transferred to the *Geschwader*.

On 7 March 1941 *Oberleutnant* Hans-Ekkehard Bob, *Staffelkapitän* of 9./JG 54, received the Knight's Cross. Born on 24 January 1917, Bob had joined the Luftwaffe in 1936 and had been present when I./JG 21 was established at Gutenfeld. He scored his first victory on 10 May 1940 and by the end of the Western Campaign had increased his total to five. By mid-November 1940, during operations over England, Bob added another fourteen victories. The successful *Oberleutnant* had assumed command of JG 54's 9. *Staffel* at the end of November. Hans-Ekkehard Bob was the fourth member of JG 54 to receive the coveted decoration.

The deployment at Le Mans came to an unexpected end for the two *Gruppen* of JG 54 at the end of March 1941. At the beginning of the year, the focus of military operations had moved to the southeast of Europe. Germany had occupied almost all of Western Europe and the English had been driven from the mainland. Except for the air war, which was winding down, at the beginning of 1941 the German armed services were not engaged in any major military operations. The same could not be said of Germany's ally in Rome. Not only had the Italians suffered only serious defeats in their African adventure, at the end of October 1940 Mussolini also launched an invasion of Greece from Albania. The offensive turned into a disaster.

The Italian defeats had brought England back to the continent, as Great Britain had sided with Greece. British troops occupied Crete and sent units to the Greek mainland. This move threatened the Rumanian oil fields. From then on the conflict entered the German sphere of interest.

In November 1940 Hitler had dispatched a unit to Rumania disguised as a training outfit. At the same time, he had assured Mussolini that he would take care of the English threat in Greece. The campaign in the spring of 1941 would also be aimed at Yugoslavia, to counter growing British influence in that country. Hungary and Bulgaria were also to take part in the war.

On 29 March 1941, as part of the German buildup, JG 54 received movement orders. Once again, they affected only the two *Gruppen* stationed in the Le Mans – Cherbourg area. I./JG 54 had moved to Jever at the end of September 1940 and had been attached to JG 1. The *Gruppe* was to remain there and defend the airspace over the German Bight.

"From Cherbourg we first flew along the Alps mountain chain to Vienna, and from there we carried on to Kezkemet in Hungary. There we were greeted by Hungarian soldiers. They wore ribbons on their headgear similar to those worn by navy personnel in Germany. The leader of Hungary at that time was Admiral Horthy. He had introduced these navy ribbons for his soldiers as a token of earlier days. Hungary had not had a navy since the end of the First World War. Because of the country's geographical situation it had no access to the sea, to say nothing of a port. But Horthy clung to his tradition. I can still see the Hungarian troops who welcomed us during our stopover, with their fluttering ribbons.

After our aircraft had been refueled, we flew to Fünfkirchen in Rumania. The entire move had taken three days. The region in which we found ourselves was largely inhabited by so-called ethnic Germans. We were given a very warm welcome. Many families invited us to dinner. These days were a very cheerful and comfortable interlude before the war again consumed us fully.

The campaign began on 6 April 1941. We took off on our first mission – providing escort for a unit of Ju 88s bound for the Yugoslav capital of Belgrade – at 06:00 in the morning.

The curious thing about our operations against Yugoslavia was that the enemy was also flying the Me 109. The Yugoslavians had purchased the aircraft from Germany some time earlier. And so Messerschmitt fighters were meeting each other in combat wearing two different national insignias.

The Yugoslavians had a total of thirty Me 109 E-3s, which were based at airfields in the Belgrade area. Only a few of them got into the air, however, and those that did not flee were shot down. *Leutnant* Ostermann was one of the pilots who succeeded in shooting down one of the Yugoslavian Me 109s on 6 April 1941. It was his ninth victory. He later noted in his diary that he now had one more victory than his chief. By that he meant me.

When I saw the Yugoslavian Me 109s in the air, it made me think back to my days at Jesau. In 1939 the Luftwaffe had trained a number of Yugoslavian pilots to fly the Me 109. One of them had been sent to Jesau and I was ordered to look after him. The Yugoslavian officer had spent fourteen days at our airfield. He was already a trained fighter pilot and I was to familiarize him with the Me 109. We spent many hours in the air together. He flew as my wingman and we flew various maneuvers. We even practiced some aerobatics.

In the evenings I would take him for a drive in the country and show him East Prussia, or we would visit a bar in Königsberg. My comrades and I spent pleasant evenings drinking with him. He was a very likeable man and spoke relatively good German. By the time he left us, we had almost developed a certain friendship between us.

All of this came back to my memory. Was this officer perhaps flying against us in one of these Yugoslavian Me 109s?

There was little anti-aircraft fire over Belgrade, but on the same day Yugoslavian bombers attacked our bases in Fünfkirchen several times. Our side even sustained losses, as several aircraft were hit. We scrambled and attacked the bombers. Our commanding officer *Hauptmann* Lignitz was able to shoot down a Blenheim in the Arad area.

On 7 April we moved to Arad in Rumania. Opposition in the air ceased after the first three days. From then on we flew low-level attacks against ground troops and supply roads. The Yugoslavian Army collapsed.

On 18 April 1941 the campaign ended and we moved from Pancevo, where we had arrived while the fighting was still going on, to the Semlin airfield near Belgrade. The Yugoslavian capital had been subjected to several heavy bombing raids, which had inflicted severe damage. After the fighting ended, several comrades and I walked through Belgrade. It was the first wrecked city I had seen with my own eyes. The people we met were completely desperate. There were also countless dogs running wild, among them beautiful Cocker Spaniels. One of them followed us the whole time, obviously hungry. Several of the men picked him up and he became our *Staffel* dog. He had a shiny coat and was coal-black, therefore we named him Negus.

After a stay of about a week at Semlin, our Me 109 E aircraft were ferried to Bucharest and given to the Rumanians. Led by the senior *Staffel* officers, the *Staffeln* flew their machines to Bucharest. The *Staffelkapitäne*, *Gruppenkommandeure* and the *Kommandeur* had to drive in service vehicles to Stolp in Pomerania. The *Geschwader* was supposed to move there to equip with the latest Me 109 F. During the drive from Belgrade to Stolp we of course took the opportunity to visit parents, wives and girlfriends. *Major* Trautloft drove via Kempten to the Allgäu,

Oberleutnant Bob via Celle to Hanover, and I via Chemnitz and Magdeburg. In Semlin the car had been packed with sausage, ham and bacon. I drove to Vienna via Arad, Szegedin and Budapest accompanied by *Oberleutnant* Bob's vehicle. There we parted ways and I drove via Prague to Chemnitz to see my fiancé. Our only overnight stop was in Budapest, where there was much to see and good food.

In Chemnitz my car spent three days being overhauled by Wanderer. I then spent a day with my parents in Magdeburg, and on the seventh day I arrived at Stolp. After converting onto the Me 109 F-2, in mid-June 1941 the III. *Gruppe* moved to Schloßberg near Insterburg in East Prussia."

8
Air War in the East

After conversion onto the new Me 109 F-2 and intensive training, in June 1941 JG 54 moved to forward airfields in East Prussia. As well, the I. *Gruppe* returned to the *Geschwader* unit. There was no flying, and much emphasis was placed on concealment.

On the German-Russian border, the Wehrmacht's buildup was almost complete. Hitler had decided to attack the Soviet Union despite the existence of a non-aggression pact.

More than 3.5 million troops, supported by armies from Germany's allies, stood ready to cross the frontier. The units were divided into three army groups: north, center and south.

JG 54 was attached to the I. *Fliegerkorps*, which was part of *Luftflotte* 1. The air fleet's mission was to support Army Group North as it advanced out of East Prussia in the direction of Leningrad. The Soviet metropolis, some 800 kilometers away, was Army Group North's objective.

"The campaign against Russia began at 03:00, early on the morning of 22 June 1941. We were stationed at Schloßberg on a forward airfield, north of Tilsit in the northeast corner of East Prussia. The aircraft were parked at the edge of a forest, camouflaged so that they could not be seen from the air.

We had only moved to the airfield a few days earlier. Our orders were to take off on our first sortie precisely at 03:00 on 22 June 1941 and fly escort for a bomber unit attacking the Russian airfields in the Kovno area. For me personally, this was an exceptionally eventful moment, at least that's how it felt to me.

We took off at the crack of dawn, and the light conditions were still marginal. Flares were supposed to be fired to signal the start of the attack, the crossing of the border into Russia.

We overflew the borderline at the assigned time. Almost immediately we saw the first flares rising, and these were followed by others. I looked to the south. As far as the eye could see, flares were rising into the sky all along the border, almost like fireworks. It was a sight I can never forget.

The border had become the front line, and white signal flares rose simultaneously along its entire length. It was the signal for the start of the war against Russia. Would our attack take the enemy by surprise, or was he expecting our attack?

Soon afterwards the sun slowly began creeping over the horizon and then quickly rose higher. The Stukas we were escorting were supposed to attack Russian airfields beyond the border. When we flew over the first airfield, the aircraft were lined up in rows as in peacetime. Most fell prey to our bombs and guns.

On that and the following days we made more attacks on Russian airfields. Sometimes we also flew low over the roads, and a number of locomotives were shot up.

Despite the apparent surprise achieved on the first day of the attack, it is my opinion that the Russians knew that our attack was coming sometime. The Russians were definitely prepared for war. History could have taken a different course if we hadn't struck first, before the Russians.

We did, however, ask ourselves why we were attacking the Soviet Union before we had achieved final victory over England. We now had a two-front war as in the First World War from 1914-1918.

I shot down my first Russian aircraft on the second day of the war, 23 June 1941. *Leutnant* Ostermann scored two victories in the same action.

Then the advance began. We drove through Lithuania in the direction of Kaunas, and then through Latvia in the direction of Daugavpils*, which was reached on 29 June 1941 (*The city is called Dünaburg in German and Dvinsk in Russian.). Our ground personnel were unable to keep pace. Each time we landed at a new forward airfield we were soon followed by two Ju 52s bringing our first and second mechanics. The remaining ground personnel followed slowly in a vehicle column, which consisted mainly of trucks. This column included our radio truck or the entire headquarters company with the workshop platoon, for example.

We had been sleeping in small tents since the start of the campaign. We had many one- or two-man tents. Some combined their tents to make a larger one. I had a small one-man tent. When we arrived at Daugavpils we set up our airfield on a large meadow on the bank along the Daugava River. When we arrived we saw that the river was in flood.

In the evening I set up my small tent. For sleeping, I had a small plank bed and a straw-filled mattress. When I was ready to go to bed, I took off my uniform and put on my pajamas. I then took off my shoes and lay down on my bed. Behind the seat of the Me 109 at head level there was a small baggage compartment capable of accommodating a small bag. That is how I came to have the mentioned items with me. I freely admit that life for us Luftwaffe personnel was rather more comfortable than it was for the infantry in the trenches.

During the night, between 02:00 and 03:00, I awoke and sensed a certain need. I sat up and slid off my bed – right into the water. My shoes and several other items floated past. What was happening?

The level of the Daugava had risen sharply during the night and our meadow, and with it all our tents, were under water. There was a great deal of loud cursing. The next day the sun dried everything out again and we continued flying our missions.

On 30 June 1941 we flew *freie Jagd* in the Dvinsk area. Russian bombers had appeared several times in recent days and had tried to slow our advance by attacking troop concentrations and roads.

My *Staffel* and I flew over a large wooded area. From the air we could see many pale brown circular patches. They were moors. Beneath us lay a huge natural moor, a completely untouched landscape. The forest was repeatedly broken by these large moors. In the center of each was a pool of water up to five meters in diameter. We could see this quite clearly from above. The trees did not grow in these places. They were surrounded by all sorts of bushes, then the ground appeared to become very soft and boggy, and finally it gave way to the pool.

As we were flying over the forest, we sighted a squadron of Russian bombers. There were twelve of them, SB-2s. These machines were very slow and relatively easy prey. My *Staffel* went to the attack and in seconds the first bomber was burning. I also shot one down on my first pass. I positioned my self behind a second aircraft. Suddenly I saw movement, and as I looked on the entire crew abandoned their aircraft and took to their parachutes. I did not see the parachutes until the moment they opened. I was somewhat surprised by this behavior. Apparently the Russians were aware of their inferiority and wanted to save their lives at least. I fired a few shots into the now unmanned aircraft, then it crashed.

When I looked around, I saw more parachutes. Apparently the crews of some of the other Russian bombers had decided to abandon their aircraft before they were shot down or had managed to bale out before they crashed. We appeared to have achieved a very fine success.

Suddenly, I saw one of the surviving bombers put its nose down, apparently in an attempt to escape by diving. I moved in behind it and pressed the firing buttons.

At such short range, my bullets immediately had a devastating effect. Fragments whirled through the air. Our height was perhaps 100 meters. The bomber faltered, touched the ground and more pieces flew off; then it began to burn, slid a little farther and finally exploded in a brilliant flash.

Moments later I saw a man nearby hanging beneath his parachute. Apparently one member of the crew had been able to bale out. I turned in his direction. The parachute was already very low. With horror, I realized that he was being blown straight toward a moor. I began circling him to see what would happen. Then the man touched down, right at the edge of the moor. But then the parachute ballooned again and the poor fellow slid about another fifty meters, causing him to end up in the wet morass. The weight of his body immediately caused him to begin sinking. He couldn't free himself and I couldn't help him. I continued circling overhead, but what could I do?

Sadly, I had to look on as the man sank into the moor, a ghastly sight. The poor fellow had escaped from his doomed aircraft, for a moment had hope that his life might be spared, and now he was going to suffocate wretchedly in this swamp. At such a moment many thoughts raced through my head, but there was no joy over the victory I had just achieved. War can be so cruel.

As soon as we returned to our airfield, I reported our success to Trautloft. The *Kommodore* congratulated me. A little later he phoned me back. Apparently he had just passed on my report of our success. Trautloft told me that *Generaloberst* Busch, the commanding general in our sector, wanted to see me. I was to give him a personal account of what had taken place. And so Trautloft and I drove to *Generaloberst* Busch's headquarters and I recounted the events of earlier in the day."

The three victories by Günther Scholz on 30 June 1941 had occurred within four minutes. *Leutnant* Ostermann was also successful, shooting down three more enemy aircraft. Altogether, the 7. *Staffel* had shot down nine of the twelve Soviet bombers.

The other *Staffeln* of the *Geschwader* had also been very successful on this day. JG 54 claimed a total of sixty-five enemy aircraft shot down on 30 June 1941. The day went down in the *Geschwader* history as the "Air Battle over Daugavpils".

During the next two weeks, Günther Scholz was able to shoot down six more Russian bombers during the fighting in the Ostrov-Pskov area, two each on the 6th and 7th of July, and one on the 10th and 12th. These raised his victory total to eighteen.

Following the success near Daugavpils, *Leutnant* Ostermann claimed three more victories on 5 July 1941 and two more one day later. He had reached the twenty victory plateau.

"Ostermann was a nice young man, but terribly ambitious. He was probably determined to earn the Knight's Cross as quickly as possible. As a result, in the air he broke all the rules.

Once, while flying escort for our bombers, we suddenly sighted an enemy formation. The enemy machines were still quite far away, their strength roughly equal to our own. Suddenly I saw Ostermann break formation. He executed a Split-S and headed straight for the enemy formation. The rest of the *Staffel* and I stayed with the bombers.

The impetuous Ostermann attacked the Russians, there was a brief turning fight, and one of the Russians went down. Ostermann had his victory and rejoined formation. The Russians were apparently so disconcerted by this cheeky behavior that they didn't pursue him. There was no further combat between us and them. We continued to escort the bombers.

After we landed I gave Ostermann hell. It wasn't the first time I had had to warn him about this. I told him that he absolutely had to follow my instructions and that he must stay in formation and carry out our mission. He replied that he had to shoot down the enemy, he had to collect victories. But we were always ordered to escort bombers or even returning reconnaissance aircraft."

"I had already mentioned the tremendous ambition of *Leutnant* Ostermann. I remember very well another unrelated incident that took place on 14 July 1941.

The day had begun very early. A wingman and I were in the air on a *freie Jagd* sortie. I really didn't have a regular wingman, and on this day I was flying with *Feldwebel* Bauch.

Not long after takeoff I spotted two tiny dots on the horizon, and soon afterwards I identified them as two Russian fighters, Ratas. These machines were by then obsolete and easy prey. We circled around and were able to position ourselves behind them without being noticed. I quickly radioed final instructions to my wingman. He would attack the one on the right, I the one on the left.

Directly behind the Rata, I pressed the firing buttons. The effects of my fire were immediate. Pieces flew off. Smoke poured out and the Rata went burning to the ground. This all happened very quickly. I turned my head to look and see if my wingman had had an equally easy time of it. At that moment I saw the Rata flitting away. *Feldwebel* Bauch did not pursue. I was so astonished by what I saw that I failed to react quickly enough. What had happened? Perhaps the *Feldwebel* had made a piloting error.

I spoke to him immediately after we had landed. *Feldwebel* Bauch hemmed and hawed. I could see that he was searching for words to explain his actions, but I found no explanation in them. I couldn't get the incident out of my head and I began mulling it over. Suddenly it came to me that Bauch had so far failed to achieve a victory during similar actions in the past weeks. The other pilots didn't like flying with him. I approached *Feldwebel* Bauch again and tried to speak to him about it.

This time I got an explanation for his behavior. He was very religious and could not bring himself to kill a man. If he fired at an enemy machine, that might happen. Well, viewed from a human standpoint this was, of course, a thoroughly admirable point of view, but for a fighter pilot it must ultimately mean death at some point.

Feldwebel Bauch was transferred soon afterwards. He left the front and went home, where he became an instructor.

On 19 July 1941, the III. *Gruppe* moved from the Ostrov area to Vereteni. On 21 July I was able to score my twentieth victory after a scramble. By doing so I matched the *Staffel's* leading scorer, as *Leutnant* Ostermann had the same number of victories at that time.

In those days one was awarded the Knight's Cross after twenty victories. Since the start of the Russian campaign I had quickly increased my total to reach this figure. *Kommodore* Trautloft came to see me. We were on a first-name basis, as we had known each other since our days together at Bad Aibling.

Trautloft told me that he had put me up for the Knight's Cross. Afterwards we talked a little about other matters. Unfortunately, I subsequently heard no more about the Knight's Cross. The requirements for the decoration were raised from twenty victories at that time. As the war went on the number became ever greater. I must honestly say that I never got to it."

Reaching a certain number of victories did not always guarantee the awarding of a decoration. There were, however, certain guidelines, and for fighter pilots the most important was the number of victories achieved. The number required for the awarding of the Knight's Cross rose as the war went on and also differed depending on the theater of war.

Until the summer of 1941 the number of victories required for the Knight's Cross was twenty. The first fighter pilots to win the Knight's Cross, for example Mölders, Galland and Balthasar, were awarded the highest decorations upon reaching this figure. Up until the start of the Russian campaign, the German fighter arm had fought western opponents exclusively.

The veterans of the Battle of Britain were able to increase their victory totals very rapidly during the first weeks in Russia. The Russian fighter pilots were less experienced and in some cases flew obsolete machines. Consequently, at the end of July the number of victories required for the Knight's Cross was increased to twenty-five, in September 1941 to thirty and in November

to forty. The figure of twenty victories was retained for those fighter pilots who remained on the Channel. It was at this time that they began treating the theaters differently.

For the pilots in Russia, the figure was raised to fifty in May 1942. For those engaged against the western allies, the figure eventually rose from thirty to forty victories.

In 1943 the number of victories required for a fighter pilot in the east to win the Knight's Cross rose to seventy-five in the spring and finally to one-hundred in the fall. Towards the end of the year, however, it was reduced again to seventy-five.

That same year saw the introduction of a point system. After the Allies launched their strategic bombing campaign, with almost daily incursions by masses of heavy bombers and their escorts, victories were assessed differently. The awarding of the Knight's Cross now required a pilot to achieve a certain number of points rather than victories. Many pilots who had achieved success on the Eastern Front also went to the Defense of the Reich. From that point at the latest, each award recommendation had to be judged on its individual merits.

Just as the requirements for the awarding of the Knight's Cross changed during the course of the war, so to did those for the higher grades of this decoration. Until about mid-1941 the Oak Leaves were awarded for forty victories. For pilots deployed exclusively in the east, this figure rose to sixty, eighty and one-hundred. In 1944 the decoration was awarded for 125 to 150 victories. For pilots in the west, from 1942 the required number was sixty to seventy victories.

In 1940 the Knight's Cross with Swords was awarded for seventy victories. For pilots deployed exclusively in the east, this number rose to 100 in 1942, to 250 in 1943, and reached its highest at 250 in early 1944, before dropping again slightly. Pilots operating exclusively in the west could receive the Swords after 100 victories.

The Knight's Cross with Diamonds, the highest decoration, was reserved for reaching special marks. Werner Mölders was awarded the Diamonds for becoming the first fighter pilot ever to reach the 100 victory mark. Adolf Galland received it soon afterwards, even though he had not quite reached that figure. Gordon Gollob received the decoration for 150 victories, Hermann Graf became the first to reach 200 and was awarded the Diamonds after 172 victories. Walter Nowotny was so decorated for 250 victories and Erich Hartmann for 300. Hans-Joachim Marseille was awarded the Diamonds for his virtuoso performance against the western allies.

In closing, it should be mentioned once again that the figures named here were only guidelines for the awarding of decorations. Other factors were considered in addition to the number of victories a pilot had achieved.

Back to the summer of 1941. Scholz's twentieth victory and *Kommodore* Trautloft's submission recommending him for the Knight's Cross coincided with the gradual increase in the number of victories required to earn the decoration. *Oberleutnant* Scholz's previous command accomplishments, such as leading the III. *Gruppe* over England, or his numerous low-level attacks, appear to have provided no additional impetus for the approval of Trautloft's recommendation.

***Major* Hannes Trautloft was himself awarded the Knight's Cross on 27 July 1941. He had scored his twentieth victory on 24 July, three days after Günther Scholz reached the same mark.**

"On the morning of 1 August 1941 my 7. *Staffel* and I moved to a small airfield near Luga. The airfield, which had just been abandoned by the Soviets, was just behind the front line. We were on alert all day long, but it wasn't until the evening that we saw action. A formation of enemy bombers flew right past our airfield. We scrambled and caught up with them. They were six DB-3 twin-engined bombers. They blindly dropped their bombs in the countryside and turned away towards the east.

I got behind one of them and fired at its starboard motor. The range was only about fifty meters. The engine began smoking and seconds later flames came out. Seeing this, I decided to break away, but something was wrong with my engine. I applied full throttle and there was a racket, as if one placed a piece of iron in a metal bowl and shook it. That didn't sound good at all.

By this time the bomber I had attacked was going down. I was alone in the air. My engine was no longer producing any power at all. My altitude was about 2,500 meters. I looked around and saw nothing but forest below me. My machine had definitely been damaged. Apparently the dorsal gunner had hit me, without my noticing it. What now? I looked keenly to the left and right. Perhaps I could land somewhere.

Suddenly, oil sprayed my windscreen, which became totally covered. Unable to see, I jettisoned the canopy. The oil continued spurting, now from both sides right into my cockpit, onto my clothing and into my face. It didn't feel hot, but it stuck to everything. When I think back on the situation now, I am struck by how amazingly calm I remained. I wasn't the least bit excited or frightened. It was, however, extremely uncomfortable.

I thought again, what should I do? Should I bale out? I had never before jumped from an aircraft. There was still the option of a belly landing. But where? Some time had passed since my initial shock, and I had become a little disoriented. I wasn't sure if I was already over the Russian side of the front. As before, all I could see around me was forest. Perhaps there was a clearing somewhere, or a land where I could risk a crash-landing.

Finally I spotted a place where there were no trees. It appeared to be a small forest plantation. There wasn't much room, but I preferred trying this to jumping from my machine. I began losing height. The motor was producing almost no power. I side-slipped to lose speed and get down more quickly. I was brushing the treetops. When I reached the small clearing I again increased my rate of descent to avoid crashing into the trees at the other end. The ground rose up quickly and I touched down quite hard. It was, in fact, a small forest plantation, and luckily the small trees absorbed some of the impact. My machine slid a short distance and then came to a stop.

My first thought was, hopefully the machine won't explode now. I had long since jettisoned the canopy, so now I had to get out as quickly as possible. I undid my parachute straps and left the aircraft. As I had no idea if a small fire might already have started somewhere, I quickly got away.

I also had no idea exactly where I was, still on the German side or in Russian territory, and there was no proper front line with infantry trenches. This was another reason why I had it in mind to get away from my aircraft and hide in the bushes.

While I was squatting down, I suddenly felt pain in my back which very rapidly got worse. Before long I could no longer stand up. Apparently I hadn't escaped the crash-landing without injury, as I was just finding out.

After about half an hour I heard voices from the forest. When they became clearer, I realized that, luckily for me, they were speaking German. I crawled out of the bushes and saw a Kübelwagen moving along a narrow forest lane not far away. I couldn't walk, so I cried out. The soldiers in the Kübelwagen saw me, stopped and came towards me. There were three men, including a *Leutnant*. They had watched our fight in the air and had also seen me come down in the forest. That was my salvation.

I was completely covered in muck. The soldiers gave me a cloth so that I could at least wipe the oil from my hands and face. The oil had run into the top of my uniform, which was completely ruined. Fortunately it hadn't been hot, only lukewarm. The slipstream had cooled it as soon as it leaked out.

One of the infantrymen went looking for my parachute, whose material was much sought after by them. Two men helped me into the Kübel and placed me in the front seat next to the driver. I told them where my base was and the Kübel drove off. I had to hold on. The seat, and of course the bumps, caused me a great deal of pain. I began a conversation with the infantrymen to take my mind off the pain. After we arrived at the airfield they dropped me off."

The pilots of the 7. *Staffel* had been anxiously awaiting the arrival of their *Staffelkapitän*. It had been an eventful flight for the *Staffel*, for *Leutnant* Ostermann had also failed to return. Ostermann later described the events from his point of view, beginning with the order to scramble, in his diary.

At this point it should be noted that the account was written at the time, probably with emotions still running high after his experience. Günther Scholz cannot recognize the Ostermann he knew in the writing. In his opinion, Ostermann turned to a bombastic description that was usually not his style.

"We were already sitting in the machines and the mechanics were hanging onto the inertia starter cranks. The engines started, and the chief was the first to take off. Then I pushed the throttle lever forward and off I went, behind the chief. The other aircraft of the Staffel took off to my left and right. Ahead of me, Feldwebel Kempf had already closed with the bomber formation and immediately shot down one bomber. Having seen our takeoff, the Soviets jettisoned their bombs, put their noses down, and headed at top speed for their own positions in Luga.

In no time the chief and I were each sitting behind a bomber. I looked around and saw fighter aircraft far behind and above us. But they must be the comrades from our Staffel! We hadn't seen any enemy fighters from the ground. So far the Bolsheviks had usually come without fighter escort. I was in firing position and pressed the buttons. We had already flown over the forward enemy lines. Below, the Soviet anti-aircraft guns had begun blazing away, when I saw flames spurt from the starboard engine of my bomber. Now he had to go down! Aim carefully again, like so, now press the buttons again…

But suddenly there was a clattering and banging in my machine! Damn, one of the bastards was shooting at me! I was about 50 meters high, had set the propeller to 12 o'clock and wound down the landing flaps to match the bomber's speed, very slow for a fighter, and was wallowing along behind the bomber. Now I could just see him past the head armor. Damned Soviet fighter! The fellow had come from above and had more speed than I. Tracers flashed by on my left and right. I quickly dove to ground level, retracted the flaps and reset the propeller pitch.

Then there was a terrific bang in my cockpit. Pieces flew off, but the kite still flew. I raced towards our lines at low level, throttle lever full forward and head back. Something must have been hit, something must be burning, for it was becoming damned hot in the cockpit. It stank terribly of scorched paint. There was no smoke coming from the radiators, so they hadn't been hit. The engine was still running at full speed, I was still roaring along at low level, the Bolshevik was still sitting behind me, albeit a little farther away. Now and then his tracer flitted past, this time left, this time right. From my own experience I knew that I offered a poor target whilst flying so low. The ground conditions and my propeller wash had to be unsettling him. He had little opportunity to aim carefully.

If I had known how badly shot-up I was! It was becoming increasingly hot in my cockpit, but the instruments showed everything normal, except the fuel. I had been in the air ten minutes at most and I had barely two-hundred liters left! Now I got it, the fellow had hit my fuel tank! The fuel was leaking out and burning! Well, I wasn't going to get far with a burning fuel tank! Naturally this realization was less than encouraging. Seconds became an eternity. The number of things one can think about in such a short time is improbably high. If only I had reached the German lines!

Aha, I was coming to the first lake. The German point troops were on the other side. Then I was over water, I had made it. Where was the enemy? He probably thought me doomed, for he had broken off his pursuit. I climbed a little. The engine was still running normally, perhaps I might even make it to the airfield. I climbed higher. I needed altitude to bale out should the crate catch fire. A belly landing was inadvisable, as the aircraft would burst into flames immediately upon landing, making it unlikely that I would get out. I climbed again, and suddenly the smoke in the cockpit thinned and then stopped almost completely. Wasn't that something? Then I was over the airfield. I lowered the undercarriage and landed immediately, as gently as I could. I hadn't lowered the landing flaps all the way, and I came in with a little too much speed. The field was large enough, however. It certainly wasn't a pretty landing, but anyway I got down in one piece. Seldom had I ever jumped from the machine so quickly.

The ground crew surrounded me. They had watched the combat from the ground and had seen my bomber go down. They showed me the thick mushroom cloud of black smoke. That's where he was, the fire was easily visible from the airfield. We immediately examined my machine. It was badly shot up. The escaped fuel had burned in the tail end of the fuselage. Everything located in the rear of the machine – radio equipment, repeater compass, etc. – was scorched. The paint on the outer skin and the rear of the baggage compartment had blistered. It had been extremely hot inside the machine. I had taken quite a few other hits too. An explosive shell from the enemy's cannon had torn holes in the canopy's Plexiglas panels. My propeller and flaps were shot up. But the engine and radiators had stayed intact. Later, when we disassembled the aircraft, we saw that, in addition to two machine-gun and one cannon strikes, the fuel tank had received an approximately seven-centimeter-long tear. That is where the fuel ran out, but then the rubber layer had resealed even this hole."

After scrambling, 7./JG 54 had shot down three of the six passing DB-3 bombers. First to score was *Feldwebel* Kempf, followed by *Oberleutnant* Scholz and *Leutnant* Ostermann. It was Ostermann's 22nd victory and also the 1,000th by JG 54. In the heat of the battle, however, he had allowed himself to be surprised by a Russian fighter and was extremely fortunate to make it back to his base. Ostermann's machine, however, was no longer fit for operations.

The consequences for *Oberleutnant* Scholz were much more serious. While shooting down his twenty-first enemy aircraft, his own machine was fatally damaged by the dorsal gunner of the doomed bomber. After a successful crash-landing, he returned injured to his *Staffel*.

"With my bad back, I was first taken to my tent. When I lay on the bed the pain at least eased a little. I then asked to send a message, first stating that I had shot down an enemy machine and second that I was no longer able to fly. I urgently needed to be examined. Before long Trautloft sent me a Bf 108, which he put at my disposal. A good friend of mine declared his willingness to fly me to Königsberg.

The Me 108 *Taifun* was a very beautiful aircraft, and every *Geschwader* had several in its complement. Sitting in it was like being in an automobile. There was a seat next to the pilot and two more behind. When we arrived at Königsberg the airfield provided a car to drive me to the hospital.

The hospital was a picture of absolute catastrophe. The rooms were filled to overflowing. Soldiers lay on the floors everywhere, some with minor wounds but also some who were badly wounded. Some had not even had their wounds dressed and were still bleeding. There were also men lying on the floor in the halls. There was certainly no room for me. I looked around a little and had my escort take me to a group of Luftwaffe personnel. I had to sit or lie down, I couldn't stand.

Soon afterwards a nursing sister came and brought me a sort of air mattress to lie on. When I had made myself a little more comfortable I looked around again. What I saw convinced me that I couldn't stay there. There was great unrest in the room, many were crying out from pain. When the duty physician arrived, I informed him that he didn't need to worry about me any more. I did, however, want to contact my *Geschwader* and ask them to again provide me with an aircraft. My parents lived in Magdeburg. If they sent me an aircraft, it could take me directly to the hospital there.

I readily admit that I enjoyed an enormous deal of personal privilege at that time. There was no way that a simple army soldier propped up against the wall opposite me could have made such a request. He had no choice but to wait until someone got to him. The doctor, however, complied with my request, and Trautloft sent word that the pilot would fly me to Magdeburg in the *Taifun*.

After my arrival there, I had my parents advised even before I left the aircraft. Then I was taken to the local hospital. X-rays revealed that I had two compressed lumbar vertebra. The affected nerves had become seriously inflamed and I spent almost four weeks in hospital. I had to remain as still as possible and was treated with massages and irradiation. My parents visited me as often as they could. My fiancé also came from Chemnitz and spent a few days in Magdeburg.

While I was lying in hospital, for the first time I had an opportunity to reflect on how the crash-landing had come about. The bomber's dorsal gunner must have scored several hits on my machine as I was attacking. He had apparently hit the engine and oil cooler located behind the propeller. I had been very fortunate that my approach to the narrow forest lane had come off relatively well. I could just as easily have crashed into the trees. It was the third incident in my life as a pilot in which I could easily have been killed.

Under treatment, my condition improved steadily and I was able to move again, though my movements were restricted at first. When I could walk again, I was released from hospital and spent a week at home with my parents. My fiancé again came to Magdeburg during this period.

I subsequently flew from Magdeburg to Berlin and from there a courier aircraft returned me to my unit. By that time the *Geschwader* had moved farther north and was based at Tsarskoye-Selo near Leningrad. On 18 September 1941 I resumed command of my 7. *Staffel*. Six weeks had passed since my crash-landing.

My back injury gives me trouble until this day. Especially now, in my old age, I sometimes have severe pain."

The preceding six weeks had been very eventful for 7./JG 54. *Oberleutnant* Gerhard Koall had taken over command of the 7. *Staffel* after *Oberleutnant* Scholz was injured. *Leutnant* Ostermann had continued adding to his victory total. On 4 September 1941, after his 29th victory, he was awarded the Knight's Cross, and soon afterward he was promoted to *Oberleutnant* with an effective date of 1 September 1941.

In the absence of *Oberleutnant* Scholz, who had repeatedly directed him to remain with his unit and not undertake individual actions during missions, Ostermann had begun putting an idea of his into practice. He began flying sorties deep into the enemy rear, accompanying only by his wingman. The other pilots of the 7. *Staffel* rejected the notion as much too risky. On 11 September 1941 they discovered to their cost just how right they were. During

one such sortie, Ostermann's wingman, *Leutnant* Peter von Malapert, was shot down and captured by the Russians.

***Leutnant* von Malapert had joined the 7. *Staffel* just before the beginning of the Russian campaign. On the successful 30 June 1941, he was shot down while flying as *Oberleutnant* Scholz's wingman. With the assistance of German flak troops he just managed to escape from his burning machine, which was upside down. Malapert scored a total of five victories before he was shot down and captured.**

Ostermann himself had by then become a true expert at dogfighting. This required great physical strength, and Ostermann, who was rather small in stature, was aided somewhat by the wooden blocks fitted to his rudder pedals. The extremely ambitious young officer was a superior pilot, and if he got on the tail of a Russian fighter he was extremely difficult to shake off. By the time *Oberleutnant* Scholz returned, Ostermann had increased his victory total to thirty-nine.

If a fighter pilot was shot down or forced to make a crash-landing and was injured, on his next mission it was important not to have thoughts that it might be his last. One had to overcome ay fears that might arise.

On 19 September 1941, two days after his return to the *Staffel*, *Oberleutnant* Scholz shot down a Russian fighter. He added two more victories on 26 and 30 September, increasing his victory total to twenty-four.

"On 30 September 1941 our *Gruppenkommandeur* Arnold Lignitz failed to return from a sortie. He had been shot down, and according to an eyewitness he had baled out over Leningrad. From that time on, nothing more was heard of him. He had either been killed in the process of being shot down or lynched by the population after landing. He had not become a prisoner, nothing to that effect was ever heard. Such news could have filtered through, even during the war. Also he was not released after the war. It must therefore be assumed that he lost his life near Leningrad on that 30 September 1941."

***Hauptmann* Lignitz had been credited with 25 confirmed victories by the time he was shot down. His successor as commander of the III. *Gruppe* was Reinhard Seiler, who later won the Knight's Cross.**

Since 12 September 1941, III./JG 54 had been based at Siverskaya. The units of Army Group North had reached their objective, the city of Leningrad, at the beginning of the month. In the preceding weeks Hitler had begun interfering with operations and when the army group reached the suburbs of the metropolis he ordered the attack to stop. Instead of conquering Leningrad,

the Wehrmacht would lay siege to the city. Other sectors of the front seemed more important to him, and so units were taken from Army Group North's sector and sent to Army Group Center for the attack on Moscow.

From that time onwards, III./JG 54 flew most of its operations over the Leningrad area, the majority of them as escorts for bomber aircraft. There were frequent air battles over the city of a million people. On 4 and 11 October 1941, *Oberleutnant* Scholz shot down two more enemy fighters, victories number 25 and 26.

With the halting of the German advance and the beginning of the siege of Leningrad, Army Group North's front became stationary. JG 54 became increasingly fragmented, its *Staffeln* scattered throughout the sector. The Soviet air force made life for the German troops increasingly difficult, and the German fighters flew numerous missions in support of the ground forces.

"Our infantry units on the Volkhov River suffered under constant attacks by Soviet fighters. The Russians would come down, strafe the roads and the infantry's trenches, and then disappear just as quickly as they had come.

We were supposed to provide fighter cover for our units and prevent these attacks to the extent possible. On 19 October 1941 we took off on one such flight. The flight to the area of operations was quite long, and the cloud cover was relatively low. We had just reached the target area and were having a look around, when three Polikarpov I-180 fighters shot out of the clouds. I immediately turned towards them and prepared to attack.

The enemy fighters had also been spotted by our anti-aircraft gunners. They appeared to be extremely nervous and immediately opened fire. Apparently it made absolutely no difference to them who it was buzzing about over their heads, for they also shot at us. From their point of view, they were simply seeing aircraft that had appeared almost simultaneously. This was of course extremely unpleasant for us.

Shortly after I turned into the three Russian fighters, I felt something hit my machine. Seconds after that, the man behind me advised that large amounts of vapor were coming from underneath. I thought it over. There was no way vapor could be coming from the underside of my machine, therefore I must have taken a hit in my undercarriage, probably the hydraulic fluid reservoir. In any case, I realized that I had been hit.

While I was still busy with my own machine, the Russians disappeared back into the clouds and the incident was over. I decided that we would head home. As we flew back, I decided to find out for sure. I advised my wingman that I would lower my undercarriage and that he should observe what happened. What he told me confirmed my suspicions. Only one undercarriage leg came down, and it only came down a little bit. The other did not move at all. I wasn't ready to give up yet. With an abrupt sideslip movement, I placed the aircraft on its side, hoping that the slipstream might force the undercarriage out a little farther. The maneuver didn't work, however. The undercarriage was jammed and refused to budge.

There was nothing left for me to do but land my machine on its crippled undercarriage as gently as possible. No sooner did I touch down, when one wingtip dug in, and the aircraft spun around and came to a stop.

I reported back to Trautloft and described what had happened. The *Kommodore* was furious and said that he was going to get hold of the anti-aircraft people and tell them to have a better look and not simply blaze away wildly into the air. They had surely cost us an aircraft. As for me, I had been lucky once again. If the 20mm anti-aircraft round had hit my cockpit, I could have been shot down and history would have been changed. I could very well have agreed with my commanding officer, but instead I calmed Trautloft. I told him we couldn't be critical of the flak. We had been flying quite close together when we flew over them and fortunately nothing more had happened."

On 2 November 1941 *Oberleutnant* Ostermann left the 7. *Staffel.* Interestingly, since *Oberleutnant* Scholz's return on 18 September 1941, he had only scored two more victories, both at the end of October.

Ostermann was transferred to 3./JG 54, commanded by *Oberleutnant* Hans Schmoller-Haldy, a friend of Günther Scholz since their days together at Bad Aibling. The 3. *Staffel* had suffered heavy casualties during the fighting in Russia and had few officers left. As well, in victories it was far behind the rest of the *Geschwader* in last place. The *Geschwader* headquarters had therefore decided to send the high-scoring Ostermann to the *Staffel* to supplement its officer corps and bolster morale. The move would prove a success. As well, Ostermann's new *Staffelkapitän* gave him much more freedom of action, allowing him to again pursue his idea of fighter sorties over the enemy rear.

Ostermann fearlessly braved enemy anti-aircraft fire and attacked the enemy wherever he found him. As a result, his score began to climb rapidly. On 9 January 1942 he shot down his fiftieth enemy machine, and on 28 January he destroyed his sixtieth. On 12 March 1942 *Oberleutnant* Ostermann was awarded the Knight's Cross with Oak Leaves, becoming the 81st recipient of the prestigious award. In January 1942 alone, Ostermann had scored fifteen victories.

Coincident with the awarding of the Oak Leaves, *Oberleutnant* Ostermann was named *Staffelkapitän* of 8./JG 54. He scored his first victory in his new position on 14 March 1942. By the end of the month he surpassed the mark of

eighty victories. Ostermann led the *Staffel* in keeping with his own concepts of fighter tactics, but he met fierce resistance from his pilots, some of whom did not want to fly with him. Ostermann himself had by then developed into a fighter pilot who could not be shaken off once he got on the tail of an enemy machine. He scored his 100th victory on 12 May 1942, however he was himself wounded in the right thigh and forearm. He just managed to return to his airfield and land his machine. Ostermann was taken semi-conscious to a nearby field hospital where he underwent emergency surgery.

In recognition of his 100th victory, on 17 May 1942 Max-Hellmuth Ostermann, *Oberleutnant* and *Staffelkapitän* of JG 54's 8. *Staffel*, became the tenth recipient of the Knight's Cross with Swords.

Ostermann was the sixth pilot in history to reach the mark of 100 confirmed victories. Werner Mölders had become the first to reach this milestone on 15 July 1941, although his victories from Spain were not included in his total. Günther Lützow scored his 100th victory on 24 October 1941, followed by Walter Oesau on 26 October. The next two were Hans Philipp on 31 March 1942 and Herbert Ihlefeld on 22 April 1942.

After recovering from his wounds, at the beginning of August 1942 *Oberleutnant* Ostermann returned to JG 54 and took back the reins of his 8. *Staffel*. Despite the serious wounds he had suffered in his last action, Ostermann clung to the idea of fighter sorties deep in the enemy's rear. On 8 August 1942, soon after returning to action, he scored his 101st victory. One day later, however, he met his ultimate fate. On 9 August 1942 Ostermann was in the air west of Amosovo, north of Velikiye Luki, with just his wingman. He was bounced from above by a Soviet Curtiss P-40 and was shot down and killed. His wingman succeeded in evading the Russian fighters. Ostermann had shot down his 102nd and last enemy aircraft before he was himself shot down. The ambitious young fighter pilot had achieved his goal of becoming one of the top German fighter aces, but in the end he paid for his ambition with his life.

The day after Ostermann left the 7. *Staffel*, *Oberleutnant* Scholz was summoned by *Kommodore* Trautloft.

"On 3 November 1941 Trautloft gave the task of searching for a Russian airfield. We were still at Siverskaya. We knew of the Russian airfield from aerial photos. It was about ten kilometers southeast of Budogost in the Volkhov sector. The area had been in German hands for several days. I was to reconnoiter the airfield and determine whether it might be usable by us. A number of army troops were placed under my command for the mission.

Riding in several Jeeps, each armed with a submachine-gun, we set out through the dark forest. I was less than enthusiastic. We didn't know if we would run into Russians, some of whom were still hiding in the woods. We found the airfield without difficulty. It was a large open area, but could probably only accommodate a single *Staffel*. We drove across the airfield and looked around. At its edge were several empty huts the Russians had used as quarters.

We drove back to Siverskaya and I reported the results of our reconnaissance to Trautloft. He subsequently ordered me to lead a flight from my *Staffel* to the airfield and land there. I was to choose my most experienced pilots, for the first landing on this unfamiliar spot would surely not be easy. We were soon in the air and shortly afterwards landed at the place. I still wasn't entirely comfortable with the whole business. I ordered my pilots to keep their engines running. If there werc still Russians about, we would have to try to get out of there as quickly as possible. I also instructed several of my pilots to stay in their aircraft at first.

I climbed out, and another pilot and I checked out the airfield and its immediate surroundings. Suddenly a *Staffel* of Me 109s appeared in the sky. I looked up and saw the aircraft form up and peel off into a dive, apparently in preparation to attack. That's all we needed!

The Me's had to be from our *Geschwader*, where else would they come from? They probably hadn't been informed of our absence. From above, all they could se was aircraft, and they probably took us for Russians. I snatched the cap from my head and began waving it. The man with me did the same.

The Me 109s must have realized who we were at the last moment. They roared low overhead and waggled their wings. I was visibly relieved."

***Oberleutnant* Scholz and his flight returned to Siverskaya. In the coming weeks the *Geschwader* occasionally used the airfield, which bore the name Grcmyatshevo on the map, as a jumping-off point for missions over the Volkhov region in the Tichvin area. It remained an uncomfortable place, however. On 5 November 1941 Soviet bombers attacked the airfield.**

On 7 November 1941 Günther Scholz was promoted to *Hauptmann*. In the weeks that followed, the number of sorties flown by JG 54 dropped. In 1941 winter arrived early and was extremely cold, even for Russian conditions.

"With the onset of winter, in Siverskaya we took up quarters in the workers settlement associated with a former Russian factory near the airfield. We lived in an area of new construction, which consisted of stoutly-built four-story houses. Each block was occupied by a *Staffel*. The *Staffel* office was located on the ground floor, while the officers and men were housed in the rooms above. It was very cold in these rooms in winter. Improvising as soldiers do in such situations, we scrounged iron stoves from somewhere and placed them in the rooms. There was plenty of wood and in this way we stayed nice and warm. The actual owners of the houses had long since disappeared.

Lake Ladoga, south of Leningrad, froze over in the last weeks of 1941. This became an advantage for the Russians surrounded in Leningrad. As soon as the ice was thick enough to bear heavy loads, it became an important supply route. Most of the traffic was at night. The Russians brought in military supplies and food over the ice.

If the weather was good and we could fly, then the lake was usually the target of our operations in those weeks. We came down low and strafed the trucks. There were frequent air battles too, as the Russians provided their columns with fighter cover. Most of the time, however, the weather was too bad for flying. Either there was fog or it snowed.

When my wife came to visit me while I was lying in hospital in Magdeburg, we had decided to marry. We had now been engaged for almost two years. I had spoken to Trautloft about it after I returned to the *Geschwader*. He suggested that I request my leave during the winter, as there probably wouldn't be so much happening then.

Now it was the deepest winter and we were snowed in on our airfield. The number of sorties had in fact dropped sharply on account of the weather. I went to the *Kommodore* and again submitted my request. Trautloft said yes and I was issued a leave pass. At that time it was still relatively easy to obtain so-called marriage leave, as long as the situation permitted.

I immediately wired my future wife and advised her that I would be arriving on the 22nd or 23rd of December. I also asked her to prepare the wedding for 27 December 1941. This caused a great deal of turmoil for my in-laws in Chemnitz, where my future wife lived and where the wedding was to take place. They had only a few days to get ready, and at the end of 1941 it was no simple thing to organize such an occasion. My mother-in-law later told me how much trouble it had caused her. The story was often told for fun later in my married life.

One minor disadvantage of a wartime marriage was the almost total absence of young people among the guests. My bride and her sisters were the youngest. All of the young men had been called up.

Our honeymoon was in Bavaria. We secured a room in a hotel and spent about a week in Munich. We subsequently returned together to Chemnitz, where my stay was unavoidably extended. Soon after our return I came down with jaundice. Friends of my in-laws had invited us to dinner. My gall bladder apparently couldn't tolerate the fatty goose they served and my illness was the result. A military doctor came to the house and I was able to recuperate in my own bed instead of in hospital. I did, however, end up infecting my wife several days later.

At the beginning of January 1942, to my surprise I received transfer orders. My days as a *Staffelkapitän* with JG 54 were over. After I had recovered from my bout of jaundice, at the beginning of February 1942 I flew back to my old *Geschwader* near Leningrad. There were still some personal effects there I wanted to collect and of course I wanted to say goodbye. I had become friends with Trautloft, his adjutants, and of course the members of my *Staffel*.

To deal with the severe cold, the *Staffel* had constructed underground bunkers for the pilots and ground personnel. They were equipped with iron stoves or home-made heaters made from gasoline cans. The bulk of the *Gruppe* was no longer in action and was reequipping on the latest version of the Me 109.

I spent a few days with JG 54, which I knew so well, and on 11 February 1942 handed command of the 7. *Staffel* to my successor, *Leutnant* Werner Pichon Kalau von Hofe. New duties awaited."

9
Air War in the North

IV./JG 1 was created in France from elements of other *Geschwader* in January 1942. While still on marriage leave, Scholz received news of his transfer to the new *Jagdgruppe* as *Kommandeur*. As a result of his jaundice and the farewell visit to JG 54 in the Leningrad area, the newly-appointed *Gruppenkommandeur* could not begin his new duties until the end of February.

In the intervening period, IV./JG 1 had taken part in the risky "Channel dash" by the battleships Scharnhorst and Gneisenau and the heavy cruiser Prinz Eugen, providing air cover for the German fleet unit. The *Gruppe* had subsequently been transferred to Jever, where its mission was to defend the German Bight against British incursions. *Hauptmann* Scholz assumed command of the *Gruppe* there on 22 February 1942.

"My days with JG 54 were over. At the time I probably said that I regretted my transfer. At least that's the way it was told after the war, and I have been asked about it more than once. I had served in JG 54 before the war, and with it took part in operations in Poland, the Western Campaign, the Battle of Britain, the

Yugoslavian campaign and the advance into Russia. I had made many friends, including the *Kommodore* Hannes Trautloft. I was of course sorry that I was forced to leave these friends and my *Staffel*.

But orders were orders. And a new and more senior position was also very exciting. When I arrived at Jever all the faces were unfamiliar. An *Oberleutnant* by the name of Rudolf Lüder introduced himself as my future adjutant. He was a reserve officer, who in civilian life had been a district administrator in Pomerania.

At Jever we continued the establishment of the hew *Gruppe* and at the same time were responsible for the so-called air defense of the German Bight. There wasn't much happening at that time, however. Now and then a few British Blenheim reconnaissance aircraft came over and fighters were scrambled. We failed to shoot down any of the enemy during this time.

It was a rather quiet time and our main business was the formation of the new *Gruppe*. More and more pilots arrived and the *Staffeln* reached their authorized strengths."

The *Staffeln* of IV./JG 1 were led by experienced officers. The 10. *Staffel* was commanded by *Oberleutnant* Diethelm von Eichel-Streiber, the 11. *Staffel* by *Oberleutnant* Hermann Segatz and the 12. *Staffel* by *Oberleutnant* Herbert Huppertz. The latter had been awarded the Knight's Cross on 31 August 1941 after his 34th victory. He had scored his fortieth victory in February 1942 during operations over the Channel.

At the beginning of March 1942, IV./JG 1 moved from Jever to Trondheim in Norway.

"As we were making preparations for our transfer flight to Trondheim, my adjutant *Oberleutnant* Lüder approached me. He told me that he was from Pomerania – which I already knew – and that his parents were living there. I noticed that he was hemming and hawing a little. Then he came out with his request. He wanted to know if we could make a slight detour during our transfer flight from Jever to Trondheim. He apparently wanted to see his family, but I told him that was impossible. The shortest route to Trondheim was due north. If we flew to Pomerania first, we would have to make a refueling stop and then our flight would have to cover a much longer stretch over the Baltic Sea. All of this for a single special request, that was out of the question.

And so we flew from Jever to Oslo, our initial destination. Gardermoen airfield, located north of Oslo, had just one runway. I was the first to land. During the approach I detected a strong crosswind. No matter, we had to land. I touched down and let the machine roll out. In the last 300 meters, my Me suddenly veered right and I tried to compensate by braking left. I was unable to keep my machine under control. It continued to veer right, and before long it was resting on its belly.

I climbed out quickly. *Oberleutnant* Lüder was next, and he was already on final approach. I waved to him. Surely he could see my machine lying at the edge of the runway. But the same thing happened to him. Well, my new command was certainly off to a fine start. The *Kommandeur* and his adjutant, both older, experienced pilots, had come to Oslo and put their machines into the grass like greenhorns.

It was an embarrassing incident, but there was no changing it now. The two of us continued our flight to Trondheim in other aircraft. Our old Me's stayed in Oslo.

The runway at Trondheim was very bad. Apparently soft ground had been used as a base. Instead of a concrete runway, the airfield consisted of two plank strips side by side. The noise on landing was considerable.

There was already more going on at Trondheim than at Jever. The English repeatedly flew up the fjord and tried to attack our ships with torpedoes. There were no bombing raids on Norwegian territory, as the country was an ally of Great Britain. The Norwegian royal house had fled to England in 1940."

On 21 March 1942, IV./JG 1 was renamed III./JG 5 and attached to JG 5 as its third *Gruppe*. The 11. and 12. *Staffel* of JG 1 became the 8. and 9. *Staffel* of JG 5. The 10. *Staffel* under *Oberleutnant* Diethelm von Eichel-Streiber became the new 1./JG 5.

7./JG 5 had been created as an independent *Staffel* on 31 December 1941 under the command of *Oberleutnant* Hans-Curt Graf von Sponeck. The *Staffel* was based at Bodö in northern Norway.

"After we had spent several weeks at Trondheim, in April 1942 we received a new transfer order. I was to take my *Gruppenstab* and the 8. *Staffel* and move to Petsamo in Finland. The II. *Gruppe* of JG 5 was already there. At the same time, the 9. *Staffel* under *Oberleutnant* Hermann Huppertz left the *Gruppe* unit, was renamed 10./JG 5 and was attached to the newly-created IV./JG 5, whose area of operations was the west coast of Norway. The 7. *Staffel* had been ordered to move from Bodö to Petsamo to take its place.

The distance from Trondheim to Petsamo was considerable. The air elements flew along the Norwegian coast via Narvik and Kirkenes to Petsamo, while the ground personnel proceeded by rail through Sweden to Rovaniemi and from there down the Arctic Ocean road to the coast.

The pilots and I flew ahead as a unit. A Ju 52 transport machine was supposed to follow. Our aircraft had to be made combat ready as soon as we got there, and to do this we needed our chief mechanics, who in turn needed some of their tools and equipment. It would be some time longer before our entire ground establishment was in Petsamo.

And so the chief mechanic of every Me 109 boarded that Ju 52. They wanted to fly all together. The aircraft was also loaded with the pilots' baggage. We always had a large suitcase of our things with us. When we moved, of course we couldn't take this baggage with us in the Messerschmitt.

When we took off, we had no idea of the dramatic turn this flight would take. En route the Ju 52 encountered fog and on 22 April 1942 flew into a mountain. Everyone on the Ju 52 was killed. The pilots also lost all their baggage, but that was of little consequence, our chief mechanics were dead.

One day later another Ju 52 was sent to Petsamo, this time with our Me 109s' second mechanics. Happily this flight was completed without incident."

At Petsamo Günther Scholz found the 7. *Staffel*, also part of his *Gruppe*, under *Oberleutnant* Hans-Curt Graf von Sponeck. Later, in July 1942, a new 9. *Staffel* was also formed, completing the III. *Gruppe*.

***Oberleutnant* Horst Carganico, the *Kapitän** of the 6. *Staffel*, was promoted to *Hauptmann* and named *Kommandeur* of the II. *Gruppe* of JG 5. (**Kapitän*, *Staffelkapitän*: commanding officer of a *Staffel*.) He had been awarded the Knight's Cross on 25 September 1941 as *Staffelkapitän* of 1./JG 77 after twenty-seven victories. His father, Viktor Carganico, was one of the pioneers of German military aviation and in 1941 had reached the rank of *Generalmajor*.**

Several days after the III. *Gruppe's* arrival in Petsamo, *Major* Gotthard Handrick assumed command of JG 5. Günther Scholz knew him from their time together in Spain, where Handrick had commanded the fighter element of the "Legion Condor". Born on 25 October 1908, Handrick's achievements in sports had made him world famous before the outbreak of war. He had won the gold medal in the Modern Pentathlon at the 1936 Olympic Games in Berlin. Previously, in 1935, he had won the European championship in the same discipline in Budapest and from 1934 to 1936 he won the German championship three times in a row.

Gotthard Handrick had commanded JG 77 since the start of the Russian campaign, and under his leadership it achieved great success in the in the southern sector of the Eastern Front. In autumn 1941 he had added two victories to go with those he had achieved in Spain. In his new capacity as *Kommandeur* of JG 5, Handrick was promoted to *Oberstleutnant*. Since its formation in January 1942, the *Geschwader* had been under the temporary command of *Oberst* Carl-August Schumacher, the *Jagdfliegerführer Norwegen. (*Commander of fighter units in Norway.)**

The present boundaries in the far north of Europe, where Norway and Russia lie next to each other, were not created until the middle of the Second World War. When Finland became independent after the fall of the Imperial Russian Empire in 1917, the country was given a direct access to the Barents Sea, the so-called Polar Sea. A corridor thirty to sixty kilometers wide separated Norway and the soon to be created Soviet Union.

After achieving its independence, Finland was rocked by a civil war. When it was over, relations with its eastern neighbor were strained by territorial demands on both sides.

After the signing of the German-Soviet non-aggression pact, the dismemberment of Poland and the annexation of the Baltic States of Latvia, Lithuania and Estonia, the Soviet Union increased its pressure on Finland. After brief, unsuccessful negotiations, on 30 November 1939 the Red Army attacked, and Finland and the Soviet Union fought a bitter war during the winter of 1939-1940.

By the end of December 1939 it had become obvious that the Red Army was incapable of quickly conquering Finland. Finland stood up to the great power, but the nation found it increasingly difficult to hold the fronts. Before this led to a collapse, on 13 March 1940 a treaty was signed and Moscow ended the war. Finland was forced to surrender some of its territory to the Soviet Union. The Finnish Corridor between the Soviet Union and Norway remained in place.

In this area were the important ore mines of the Petsamo region. Petsamo itself, the largest town in the corridor, had just under 2,000 inhabitants. The terrain was almost exclusively hostile tundra. Nevertheless, the area played a major role in German planning for a campaign against Russia.

After the occupation of Norway, Germany was able to win Finland over as an ally for the coming campaign. The Finns saw it as an opportunity to regain the territories they had lost to the Soviets. Finland allowed German troops passage through their territory and later committed powerful units in the war against Russia.

The XIX. *Gebirgskorps under the command of *General der Gebirgstruppen* Eduard Dietl went into position on the Norwegian border with northern Finland. (**Gebirgskorps*: mountain corps) Its mission was to guard the area around Petsamo and capture the Soviet metropolis and port city of Murmansk, about 100 kilometers away.**

The attack on Murmansk began on 29 June 1941. After a few days the German offensive bogged down at the Liza River, about fifty kilometers from Murmansk. Unlike the German advance farther south into the seemingly end-

less expanses of Russia, after a few weeks the war north of the Arctic Circle settled into positional warfare. The front lay almost exactly halfway between Petsamo and Murmansk.

Nothing had changed by the time III./JG 5 arrived at the end of April 1942. A bitter war was waged in the tundra in scarcely-imaginable climatic and geographical conditions. Now the German fighter pilots had to come to grips with these conditions too.

"The most important objective of the front in the north remained Murmansk. The city had the only large port that remained completely ice-free in winter, as the bay was affected by the Gulfstream. Thus Murmansk became one of the most important destinations for the Allied convoys, which had been delivering materiel to support the Red Army since the summer of 1941. From the port city the aid deliveries travelled down the Murmansk railway to the fronts in the south.

We often escorted Stukas during their attacks on ships in Kola Bay. The coast there was very rocky and steep. Below lay the port of Murmansk, flanked on the left and right by anti-aircraft guns sited on the surrounding hills. The Stukas dove towards the bay and we had to follow, as the Russian fighters also buzzed over the bay. On one such flight I got a Russian as he was about to get on the tail of a Ju 87. These dive-bomber missions to Kola Bay were very uncomfortable on account of the anti-aircraft guns, which were situated relatively high up on the hills.

There were also bomber units based in the Petsamo area, including some torpedo bombers. It was their job to attack the convoys at sea and ships in the port of Murmansk. We also had to fly escort for them. And so our missions either took us over the ice-cold sea or the city of Murmansk with its heavy flak defenses.

Later, from the spring of 1943, our *Geschwader* had its own *Jabo-Staffel**, 14./JG 5, led by *Hauptmann* Strakeljahn. It accounted for a considerable number of enemy ships sunk. (**Jabo*, short for *Jagdbomber*: fighter-bomber)

Operating far out over the sea, our reconnaissance aircraft provided timely warning of Allied convoys approaching Murmansk. If the convoy was within range, we took off to attack. The early convoys sailed relatively close to the coast of Norway as they headed for Murmansk. They regularly came under attack from our bombers with fighter escort, however, and soon they began sailing farther to the north, trying to stay beyond our range for as long as possible. On the final leg of their voyage they sailed almost straight south in the direction of Murmansk. We were left with less time to attack the convoys, as we always had to factor in our return flight.

At the latest, the convoy came within range when it entered Murmansk Bay. These attacks were not always intercepted, but very often there were combats with

Russian fighters. Generally we hated the flights out over the open sea, and I'm not just speaking for myself here. Sometimes we flew far in excess of 100 kilometers, and of course we had to fly the same distance back. If we saw nothing during the entire flight but the cold Polar Sea, then the nervous strain was enormous. Even in summer the Barents Sea, which was its proper name, was rarely warmer than seven degrees. If one was forced to ditch in this icy water, hypothermia was certain within fifteen minutes at latest. We wore the same equipment as during the flights over England, including the yellow dye pouch, which made it easier for the air-sea rescue crews to spot us.

On the Channel this was all very nice. The Channel was barely thirty-five kilometers wide and there were air-sea rescue aircraft and rescue vessels. While these were sometimes attacked by the English, at least they were still there. If one ditched in the Channel, at least there was the possibility of rescue.

Things were very different in the Polar Sea. The only port that would have been available to us was Kirkenes in Norway. I cannot remember seeing rescue vessels during my time there. It may be that some air-sea rescue aircraft were active, but I don't think they ever found anyone in time. Thank God little happened during the time of our missions over the sea. None of my people were forced to come down in the sea during my time as *Gruppenkommandeur*.

The missions to Murmansk were different again. The flight to Murmansk was also quite long, but it was over land. Below us lay the tundra. Such growth as there was, was limited to small birch woods. At this latitude the birches were no taller than two to three meters. It looked very pretty in summer, but in winter the tundra was a barren landscape. The lakes were frozen over, which was an advantage, as one could walk across them. There were frequent air battles over Murmansk and also on the flights there and back. Now and then one of our pilots was forced down. There were many who were shot down and then made their way home on foot across the tundra. This was a tremendous feat in winter. Sadly, there were also many who failed to make it back.

We dressed warmly for our flights. In addition to fur boots and vests, we also wore fur gloves and caps for our ears, into which our headsets were fitted. Sometimes, after baling out, the jerk of the parachute opening would cause a pilot to lose his fur boots if they weren't tied tightly enough. He then found himself on the ice of the tundra in his sock feet. This happened to Horst Carganico, for example.

Sometimes people walked for three days before they reached the thin lines of the German mountain troops. There they were given food and medical treatment. Usually their feet were frozen.

If one was forced to walk through the tundra in summer, when it was warm, the lakes were no longer frozen and one had to cover greater distances. The flies were also most unpleasant then. On our belts we always carried a bottle of liquid, which we could spray onto our skin and rub in to protect us from this plague. Sometimes during our hours off in Petsamo, the only protection was to wear a bug net over one's face.

For combat missions, in addition to the fur articles previously mentioned, one wore overpants, so-called Channel pants, with leg pockets in which rations were stowed. On the belt we carried a pistol, a folding knife and, in summer, the previously-mentioned bottle of fly dope for protection against the mosquito plague in the tundra. We also carried the mosquito net with us. Also in the aircraft was a rucksack with food and a sleeping bag. In the parachute rucksack there was more food and another sleeping bag in case one had to bale out. In winter there were also skis in the aircraft.

There was more to get used to in the far north besides climatic conditions. In summer we had to get used to the perpetual daylight, when the sun never went down. At twelve midnight it was still a good two hands above the horizon. At that time cockpit or alert readiness was always laid on, or missions were also flown.

In winter, on the other hand, for several months the sun never came up, never rose above the horizon. During the day the sky was gray and the maximum light conditions were equivalent to the early dawn. During this period it was impossible to fly morc than two missions a day. It was possible to fly during the twilight period, as one could see the ground. But from 15:00 hours until early noon darkness reigned. We used the time to catch up on our sleep or passed the time in other activities.

There was no point in trying to do something to the machines, as it was always dark. One cannot praise the accomplishments of the ground personnel often enough. Whether it was the aircraft mechanic, the armorer or the radio technician, if an aircraft returned damaged from a mission, the ground crew had to have it serviceable again for the next day, summer or winter. Sometimes they had to work in light from vehicle headlamps and the deepest cold. Their work was often very uncomfortable.

The winter brought with it hard physical labor, especially for the ground crews. They had to go out to the machines during the night, many hours before the first mission, to try to get them ready for flight. The engines were covered with a cloth blanket. A vehicle was pulled up beside each aircraft, and it blew warm air through a hose into this cover to warm the engine at least a little. Without this preparation they had no chance of getting it going. Nevertheless, very often the engine did not start immediately. When this happened, an electric motor was employed to turn the inertia starter.

Another labor-intensive task was moving the aircraft about the airfield and camouflaging them. The aircraft were parked in blast pens, which protected them from bomb fragments. In winter snow was shoveled against the outside walls of the pens, providing instant camouflage.

The Russians built entire fake airfields and wooden mock-ups of their various aircraft types. From above they looked like real aircraft. I personally saw several of these dummy airfields. In winter they, too, built pens for their aircraft and camouflaged them with snow. They forgot one thing, however. If the aircraft were real, they produced clouds of snow when the engines were started. The propeller blew the snow away and the ground was darker in the places where the aircraft exited the pen. We could see this from the air. If no such signs were present, we dropped down, had a look around and quickly identified the mock-ups.

Of my personal victories during my time with JG 5, I have no particular memories of dogfights. Most of our engagements took place in the Murmansk area. When we flew home, the Russians usually didn't follow us very far."

Günther Scholz had scored his first victory in the far north and as *Gruppenkommandeur* on 28 April 1942, when he shot down a Hurricane. On 18 May 1942 he shot down another Hurricane 20km west of Murmansk. He had long since become an experienced tactician in aerial combat, having flown several hundred sorties in the previous years. Increasingly, he came to regard his job as *Kommandeur* as successfully leading his pilots in the air and the *Gruppe* as a whole.

One of JG 5's most successful pilots in the summer of 1942 was Rudolf Müller. Born in Frankfurt am Main on 21 November 1920, he had joined 1./JG 77 as an *Unteroffizier* in September 1941. On his very first day of operations from Petsamo, Müller flew three sorties, and on 12 September 1941 he scored his first victory. At the beginning of 1942 1./JG 77 became 6./JG 5. By then Müller had increased his victory total to ten.

His most successful period began at the end of April 1942 when he returned to Petsamo. Müller shot down five enemy aircraft on 23 April and ten more by the end of the month. In May 1942 he scored thirteen more victories. On 2 June 1942 he shot down two Hurricanes to increase his total to forty victories. On 19 June 1942, *Feldwebel* Rudolf Müller was awarded the Knight's Cross in recognition of his success. By then he had shot down a total of forty-six enemy aircraft. Müller was the first member of JG 5 to be awarded the Knight's Cross.

Rudolf Müller's successful career as a fighter pilot came to an abrupt end on 19 April 1943. Since promoted to *Oberfeldwebel*, on that day he failed to return from a combat mission. Müller was shot down in an engagement near Murmansk and made a successful forced landing. He was able to retrieve his

skis and set out for the front lines, however he was captured by Soviet troops. At that point his trail vanished.

Officially, Rudolf Müller died in a Soviet prisoner of war camp on 21 October 1943. When he was shot down, his total stood at ninety-four confirmed victories, making him the most successful German fighter pilot in the far north, and he was about to be awarded the Knight's Cross with Oak Leaves.

In the summer of 1942 the members of the *Geschwader* flew a constant series of missions, most of them in the Murmansk area. *Hauptmann* Scholz added two victories to his total during this period. On 14 July 1942 he shot down a Soviet Hurricane fighter in the Murmansk area and on 12 August he downed a MiG-1 near Ura-Guba, a town on the coast of the Barents Sea northwest of Murmansk.

Günther Scholz had achieved his thirtieth confirmed victory during the Second World War, and on 8 September 1942 he was awarded the German Cross in Gold. A few days earlier, on 23 August, the Finns had awarded him the Finnish Freedom Medal, Third Class.

A sequence of photographs was taken after Scholz returned from the mission in which he scored his thirtieth victory, and they are reproduced in the photo section.

At the beginning of October 1942, *Hauptmann* Hans-Curt von Sponeck, the *Staffelkapitän* of 7./JG 5, was ordered to the Luftwaffe Officer Candidate School in Berlin-Gatow to attend a unit leader's course. Before he could depart, however, his name was removed from the list of course participants. He learned the reason soon afterwards. It had nothing to do with his person, rather with his name.

When the war broke out, his father, Hans von Sponeck, was a *Generalmajor* in command of the 22nd Infantry Division (Air Landing). After the Polish campaign, in February 1940 he was promoted to *Generalleutnant.* For his actions at the beginning of the Western Campaign and his division's success in Holland, on 14 May 1940 he was awarded the Knight's Cross.

After the invasion of the Soviet Union, on 10 October 1941 *Generalleutnant* von Sponeck assumed command of the XXXXII Army Corps. He and his corps assumed a defensive posture on the coast of the Kerch Peninsula.

On 26 December 1941 the Red Army conducted landings on the peninsula, as a result of which elements of the XXXXII Army Corps were placed in danger of being cut off. On 29 December *Generalleutnant* von Sponeck issued orders for his 46th Infantry Division to retreat, saving many soldiers from death or captivity.

Developments on the entire Eastern Front had led Hitler to issue a *Führer* Order on 26 December 1941, forbidding retreats without his prior approval. *Generalleutnant* von Sponeck was unaware of this order when he made his decisions. Nevertheless, he was relieved of his command for this "unauthorized" withdrawal. From *Führer* Headquarters came orders that *Generalleutnant* von Sponeck was to face a court martial in Berlin to answer for his actions.

Reichsmarschall Hermann Göring personally presided over the trial. The accused *Generalleutnant* was forced to stand throughout the proceedings and important witness statements were not allowed. On 23 January 1942, Hans von Sponeck was sentenced to death for gross insubordination in the field. Hitler wanted to make an example of this general.

Following an appeal to Hitler by *Generaloberst* Curt Haase, on 20 February 1942 the sentence was commuted to six years imprisonment. Hans von Sponeck began serving his sentence in Germersheim fortress prison on 6 March 1942.

These events had caused the name of Sponeck to fall into disfavor in senior Luftwaffe circles, something Hans-Curt von Sponeck soon came to realize. After his orders to report to the Officer Candidate School had been cancelled, his time as a *Staffelkapitän* in JG 5 also came to an end. While *Hauptmann* von Sponeck was trying to find an explanation for what was happening to him, *Hauptmann* Hans-Hermann Schmidt took over 7./JG 5 in an acting capacity.

Hans-Curt von Sponeck returned to the *Geschwader* at the beginning of December 1942, however just a few days later he officially handed command of his 7. *Staffel* over to his successor *Oberleutnant* Gerd Senoner. Von Sponeck was then transferred to *Schnellkampfgeschwader* 10 based at Caen. His father could no longer help him.

Although *Generalleutnant* Hans von Sponeck had nothing to do with the events of 20 July 1944, on 23 July 1944 he was shot in Germersheim by personal order of Heinrich Himmler.

After the unpleasant events surrounding the meritorious *Kapitän* of the 7. *Staffel*, in mid-November 1942 III./JG 5 had reason to celebrate. On 13 November 1942 *Feldwebel* Heinrich Bartels became the *Gruppe's* first recipient of the Knight's Cross.

Born in Linz, Austria on 13 July 1918, Bartels had volunteered for service in the Luftwaffe in 1939 and in May 1941 joined JG 26 "Schlageter" as a *Gefreiter*. Bartels scored his first victory on the Channel Front on 19 August 1941 and his second on 27 August. At the end of January 1942 he was transferred to 11./JG 1, which later became 8./JG 5.

As an *Unteroffizier* and later a *Feldwebel*, Bartels became one of the 8. *Staffel's* most successful pilots. In September 1942 alone he recorded twenty-one victories. For his success, Bartels was awarded the German Cross in Gold on 20 October 1942 and the Knight's Cross on 13 November 1942. By the time he received the Knight's Cross he had increased his victory total to forty-five.

Heinrich Bartels scored four more victories in the far north before he was transferred to JG 27 in spring 1943. At the beginning of October 1943 he began a new series of victories over southeastern Europe. By mid-November 1943 the experienced dogfighting specialist had scored twenty-four victories over aircraft flown by the Western Allies. From April 1944 he operated successfully in the Defense of the Reich and over the invasion front. By the end of June 1944, Bartels had increased his victory total to ninety-six.

Following promotion to *Oberfeldwebel*, Bartels again flew in the Defense of the Reich. On 23 December 1944 he scored his 99th victory but was then shot down by an American Thunderbolt pilot. After more than 500 combat missions, Heinrich Bartels met a flier's death in the Bonn area. As one of the most successful pilots against western opponents, he had been recommended for the Oak Leaves, however he did not live to receive the decoration. Bartels went down in a remote wooded area and the remains of pilot and aircraft were not found and recovered until 1968.

By the time Heinrich Bartels was awarded the Knight's Cross in November 1942, the number of missions being flown by JG 5 had dropped significantly compared to the summer. The *Geschwader* experienced its first winter north of the Arctic Circle. There were only a few hours each day in which missions could be flown. The rest of the day the men of JG 5 battled the cold and darkness. The *Kommodore* saw to it that boredom didn't set in during those periods with no action.

"Gotthard Handrick was a very nice and approachable man, and he was a great sportsman. His sporting activity expressed itself in Petsamo too. In winter, for example, he ordered us to go skiing. If no missions were possible, then it was on with our skis and once around the airfield, with Handrick himself always in the lead. One such circuit took about an hour. Making us exercise was of course the right thing to do, but we were too lazy to enjoy it as we should have.

Afterwards there was cod liver oil to drink, another idea from our *Kommodore*. This was important for the vitamins it provided. We very rarely had fresh fruit and vegetables. Everything was frozen, but necessity is the mother of invention.

An example of this is the process involving our potatoes. They stayed in the open throughout the winter and were frozen hard. The cooks shoveled them out and dropped them into their metal buckets with a clang. I watched this once. I knew that if potatoes were frozen and then thawed out, the result was a mush that was totally uneatable. I went to the cook and spoke to him about it. He suggested that they pour boiling water over the potatoes. This would thaw them out quite suddenly and quickly, making them taste like normal boiled potatoes. This was one of the small tricks used by the people responsible for our daily routine. The common soldier expected to be supplied with good rations, but sometimes this wasn't so simple.

To provide ourselves with fresh meat we turned to a rather unusual method. Moose were quite plentiful in the far north. We could see their tracks in the snow when we flew over the tundra. The Finns hunted these animals on skis, sometimes chasing them for days until the moose had literally run themselves to death. That was out of the question for us.

We used our Fieseler Storch to hunt moose. With this machine we could land anywhere, in open terrain or on frozen lakes. In winter, skis replaced the wheeled undercarriage. We flew over the tundra in the Storch, followed the tracks in the snow and then shot at the moose from above with submachine-guns. It wasn't very sportsmanlike of course, but effective. Afterwards we landed right beside the animals. We had an *Oberleutnant* who was a professional hunter. He always took part in these "hunting sorties" and butchered the animal on the spot. A moose provided a lot of meat, which tasted wonderful. Each animal provided enough for the entire unit to enjoy roast moose or a good soup for almost a week.

The Fieseler Storch also rendered valuable service in rescuing pilots who had been shot down or had force-landed and were out in the tundra somewhere waiting for help.

Our sportsman Gotthard Handrick wanted us to be prepared for such situations. He came up with the idea that every pilot should have to spend one night in an igloo. The Finns showed us how such an igloo was built. There were several ways of accomplishing this. One either heaped up a solid pile of snow and then burrowed into it, or constructed a dome using precut snow squares. The important thing was that one created a hole in the igloo in which one could stay.

Every pilot carried a candle with him when he went on a mission. Once inside the igloo, one closed off the entrance and lit the candle. This was sufficient to produce a comfortable degree of warmth. Handrick ordered that everyone should construct one such igloo and spend a night in it."

Hans von Hahn had worn the Knight's Cross since 9 July 1941. Like Günther Scholz, he had joined the navy as a cadet in 1934 and in 1935 entered the Luftwaffe. When war broke out he was *Staffelkapitän* of 8./JG 53 and his *Kommandeur* at that time was Werner Mölders. Hans von Hahn scored his first victory on 22 December 1939 and he added six more during the Western Campaign. He assumed command of I./JG 3 on 27 August 1940 and scored six more victories over England and the Channel.

After the invasion of the Soviet Union, von Hahn quickly reached the twenty victory mark, which earned him the Knight's Cross. In September 1941 I./JG 3 moved back to the west and was later renamed II./JG 1. At that time Hans von Hahn had thirty-four confirmed victories.

In May 1942 Hans von Hahn was transferred to the headquarters of JG 5. He remained with the *Geschwader* until the beginning of January 1943 and was subsequently assigned to the staff of the *General der Jagdflieger*. Then in July 1943 he became *Kommodore* of JG 103 and in the final months of the war he took over the post of *Jagdfliegerführer Oberitalien. (*Commander of fighter units in Northern Italy)**

"In the autumn of 1942 *Hauptmann* Gerhard Wengel had turned command of the 9. *Staffel* over to *Oberleutnant* Wulf-Dietrich Widowitz.

Widowitz was a temperamental, one could say rather over-refined young man, who was the source of much bad feeling. He was always on bad terms with someone. There was one incident involving the then *Feldwebel* Walter Schuck in which shots were even fired. That was, of course, too much, and I had to step in and make peace between the two.

I have one particularly vivid memory involving Widowitz. The duration of the war brought me a completely new duty as *Kommandeur*. In February 1943 I performed a so-called long-distance wedding for *Oberleutnant* Widowitz.

A photograph took the place of the bride during the ceremony, and the groom put on his best uniform. I gave the usual speech in the name of the *Führer*, and after this brief ceremony the man and woman were officially married.

The usual reason for such a long-distance marriage was that the bride was pregnant and the groom was unable to get leave for a proper wedding. Had he been killed later in the war, the woman would have had an illegitimate child.

Wulf-Dietrich Widowitz was in fact killed during a flight in the summer of 1943. He went down behind the lines in a Gotha Go 145. On 31 August 1943 he was awarded the German Cross in Gold posthumously in recognition of his 36 victories.

Widowitz was not the only one for whom I had to perform a long-distance wedding. Several months later I married another enlisted man from the *Gruppe*."

"Our airfield at Petsamo was often attacked by Russian Il-2s. These attacks always caught us by surprise. The so-called *Schlächter*"* came at low level, just skimming over the hills, and attacked the airfield. (*Short for *Schlachtflugzeg*, or close-support aircraft.) Sometimes they inflicted quite a lot of damage, dropping bombs and strafing with their machine-guns. Fortunately, we suffered few casualties in personnel, but now and then our aircraft and installations were damaged.

We were rarely able to prevent these attacks. As they came in low, our radar warning service was unable to detect and report them. We were unable to take off in time to intercept. A scramble after they appeared over the airfield was rarely successful, for by the time we got airborne the Russians had disappeared. It wasn't far to the tundra, and they flew home untouched across the vast, unpopulated wasteland.

Occasionally, however, our aircraft were already in the air when the attack came, or we received adequate warning to take off from the airfield in time. One such occasion was on 5 March 1943. We were barely airborne when they came, at very low altitude as always. There was a brief battle in which I shot down one of the attacking Il-2s.

After our airfield had been attacked several times, I obtained a 20mm anti-aircraft gun from the light flak battalion responsible for the defense of the airfield. I had them show me how to use the gun, practiced a little, and then had it set up right next to my command post. It was more a joke, anything to avoid sitting idly by while our airfield was being attacked. The gun beside the door was subsequently used quite often, provided there was someone nearby who could operate it when the attacks came.

One day it was I who was nearby when, late in the afternoon, several Il-2s suddenly flew over the field at low level. I ran to the anti-aircraft gun and opened fire. It was no simple matter for an untrained gunner to score hits, but I was able to see my shells striking the Il-2 I was aiming at. But nothing happened, and it flew merrily on its way. My hits had no effect on the armored close-support aircraft. After the Russians had dropped their bombs they disappeared again. We had failed to shoot down any of them."

10
Kommodore

"At the end of May 1943 Gotthard Handrick left the *Geschwader* to take over new duties. In September 1943 he was named *Jagdfliegerführer Ostmark* and while serving in that post he was promoted to *Oberst* on 1 October.

I was the senior *Gruppenkommandeur* in JG 5 and on 1 June 1943, just three months after my promotion to *Major*, I was placed in command of the *Geschwader*. This did not meant hat I was named *Kommodore*, however.

From then on my superior was the *Fliegerführer Nord* (*Ost*). At the time I assumed command, this was still *Generalmajor* Alexander Holle, whom I knew very well. Sometimes I also received my operational orders directly from senior officers in the Luftwaffe command.

As time went by, as leader of the *Geschwader* I took part in fewer and fewer operational sorties. As I saw it, my responsibilities lay in the command and organization of the unit, even more so than when I was a *Gruppenkommandeur*. As well, operations were now flown by a single *Gruppe* at most. *Geschwader*-strength operations by JG 5 were never possible.

Stationed at Petsamo were the *Geschwaderstab*, the II. *Gruppe* and my old unit, the III. *Gruppe*. Several *Staffeln* were regularly rotated to south-central Finland. The I. and the IV. *Gruppe* of JG 5 were based in Norway and operated from airfields scattered along the coast. I had no contact at all with them. Later I./JG 5 was even sent to France and the Defense of the Reich.

Jagdgeschwader 5 was thus rather split up and I commanded just two *Gruppen*. Our area of operations consisted exclusively of the area between Kirkenes and Murmansk and from the coast down to central Finland as far as Alakurtti.

In the summer of 1943, operations against Allied convoys bound for Murmansk remained the focal point. At the same time, the Russians intensified their attacks on our supply convoys to Kirkenes, which affected us at Petsamo. We fought bitter air battles and foiled many of these attacks."

On 1 June 1943, the day Günther Scholz was placed in command of the *Geschwader*, *Hauptmann* Heinrich Ehrler was named the new *Kommandeur* of III./JG 5. He had previously led the 6. *Staffel*, an extremely successful unit.

Born on 14 September 1917, Heinrich Ehrler joined the Luftwaffe in 1935 and took part in the Spanish Civil War as an anti-aircraft gunner. He began training as a pilot in January 1940 and was subsequently attached to

4./JG 77 on the west coast of Norway as a *Leutnant*. It was there that Ehrler scored his first victory.

On 1 February 1941 4./JG 77 became 4./JG 5 and the *Staffel* had meanwhile moved to airfields in Finland and northern Norway. *Leutnant* Ehrler increased his victory total to eleven before moving to 6./JG 5. There he was named *Staffelführer on 22 August 1942, by which time he had achieved fifty-five victories. (**Staffelführer*: literally "*Staffel* leader". An officer who performed the functions of a *Staffelkapitän* but had yet to be officially confirmed in that position.) On 4 September 1942 he was awarded the Knight's Cross, by which time his victory total stood at sixty-four.**

Heinrich Ehrler continued his successful ways, and he was promoted to *Oberleutnant* and then to *Major*. By 1 June 1943, when he succeeded *Major* Günther Scholz as *Kommandeur* of III./JG 5, he had become the most successful pilot in JG 5. On 8 June 1943, just a few days after becoming *Kommandeur*, Ehrler scored his 100th victory. He was the first fighter pilot in the far north to reach this milestone, and on 2 August 1943 he became the first member of JG 5 to win the Oak Leaves after his 112th victory.

As previously mentioned, as leader of the *Geschwader* Scholz was in constant contact with the *Fliegerführer Nord* (*Ost*). The position of *Fliegerführer Nord* had been created in March 1941 and in December 1941 had been split into a *Fliegerführer Nord* (West) and a *Fliegerführer Nord* (*Ost*). The first *Fliegerführer Nord* (*Ost*) was *Oberst* Alexander Holle, who was promoted to *Generalmajor* on 1 February 1943 and decorated with the German Cross in Gold on 26 May 1942 and the Knight's Cross on 23 December 1942. On 7 June 1943 *Generalmajor* Holle handed his post over to *Generalmajor* Ernst-August Roth, who was succeeded by *Oberst* d.R. Dr. Ernst Kühl in August 1943. On 6 November 1943 *Generalmajor* Roth was also awarded the Knight's Cross for his service as air commander in the far north.

***Oberst* Dr. Kühl already wore the Knight's Cross when he took over his new post of *Fliegerführer*. He had earned the decoration, which was awarded to him on 17 October 1942 as an *Oberleutnant der Reserve*, for his actions as *Kommodore* of KG 55 "Greif". He had also been awarded the German Cross in Gold on 21 August 1942. On 18 December 1943, several months after his transfer to the Polar Sea Front, Dr. Kühl was also awarded the Knight's Cross with Oak Leaves for his success as commander of KG 55.**

***Major* Günther Scholz took part in the transfer of command from *Generalmajor* Ernst-August Roth to *Oberst* d.R. Dr. Ernst Kühl in August 1943.**

All units and commands of the German air force in Norway and Finland were attached to *Luftflotte* 5. The commander of this air fleet was

***Generaloberst* Hans-Jürgen Stumpff, who had held the position since 10 May 1940. Günther Scholz has vivid memories of a meeting with the commander of *Luftflotte* 5 in Oslo.**

"*Generaloberst* Stumpff had called a large conference in Oslo. The air fleet staff was quartered in the former Hotel Holmenkollen. As I went up the stairs, I was approached by a naval officer whom I knew from somewhere. It was *Kapitänleutnant* Bloser, our instructor from the naval school in Mürwick. He now wore the insignia of a *Fregattenkapitän**. (*German naval rank equivalent to Commander)

I said to the man, "Hello, *Herr Kapitän*. Remember me?" He looked at me and replied, "Yes, I think so. But I can't recall your name." "I am Scholz, I was in Crew 34." Then he smiled at me. "Of course. Scholz from Crew 34. Those were pleasant days we spent together."

We talked for a few minutes and then said goodbye, for I had to go to the conference. I later learned that after his tour as an instructor in Mürwick, Wilhelm Bloser had served on the light cruiser "Leipzig" from 1937 to 1940. He had subsequently served as a group leader in naval operations until summer 1943 and was now *Luftflotte* 5's naval liaison officer.

I don't remember exactly what the conference was about. *Generaloberst* Stumpff had summoned to Oslo almost all of the Luftwaffe commanders from his area. The actual talk was given by the chief-of-staff. Afterwards, various commanding officers were called into the air fleet commander's office for further instructions. I was among those he wanted to speak to.

Stumpff sat at a large desk, which was on a carpet of pure wool. The *Generaloberst* looked very nervous and unsettled. During our conversation he was constantly shuffling his feet beneath the desk. When we were finished, Stumpff stood up, came toward me and extended his hand. Before our hands touched, a spark leapt from him to me. At first we were quite shocked, but then we looked at each other and had to laugh. Stumpff said, "Am I really that charged up?"

I told him that the wool carpet was probably responsible. Stumpff was wearing boots with leather soles. The constant rubbing of his feet on the carpet had built up a large electrostatic charge, which he passed to me."

In the summer of 1943 the units of JG 5 based in the Petsamo and Kirkenes area flew several missions almost daily. The 18th of August 1943 was no different. In the afternoon the *Stab* of III./JG 5, along with the 8. and 9. *Staffel*, took off on a mission against Russian supply vessels sailing north along the east coast of the Fischer Peninsula. The attack force consisted of Fw 190 fighter-bombers and Me 109 escort fighters.

***Major* Scholz, the *Geschwader* commander, took part in the operation. Once they had reached the target area, he and his wingman assumed the role of high cover. While the *Jabos* attacked the Soviet supply ships, the Me 109s became involved with the Russian fighters flying cover.**

From his position, *Major* Scholz observed the progress of the air battle. As he watched an Me 109 enter a cloud bank as it gained altitude for another attack, he saw a Russian fighter climbing up behind it. Scholz saw his opportunity and began to descend. He fired a burst that struck the Russian machine, a Kittyhawk fighter, as it emerged from the cloud bank. *Major* Scholz had scored another victory.

Back at Petsamo, the operation was judged a success. Günther Scholz and several other pilots claimed victories and the *Jabos* had scored hits on the enemy ships.

Despite all these local successes, however, there were growing doubts as to the worth of these operations. There were air battles almost every day, and the victory totals rose steadily, but many members of JG 5 also failed to return.

The situation on the Eastern Front had long since turned against the Germans. In the far north, they tried to form their own picture of what was happening.

"We listened to Radio London, of course, and the reception up there was wonderful. In this way we were always able to form our own ideas as to how the war was going. It was particularly bad at the time of the lost battle at Stalingrad. Our radio had given an extremely sanitized version of what was happening, but Radio London revealed the true scope of this drama.

Within our small community, by then we were all agreed that we could no longer win the war. We thought that perhaps we could still get out of it relatively unscathed, but not win in the actual sense.

We could see with our own eyes that our enemies were growing ever stronger. The convoys we attacked were delivering countless thousands of aircraft, trucks and tanks to the Russians. Down the vital Murmansk railway, these deliveries travelled to the Leningrad front and deeper into Russia."

JG 5 began its second winter above the Arctic Circle. In 1943 the front outside Murmansk had become stationary, and neither side had been able to achieve a decisive advantage.

"One time I had to go to Rovaniemi for a meeting at the headquarters of the *Fliegerführer Nord* (*Ost*). Flying was out of the question on account of the prevailing

Polar night. There was a sort of twilight between 11:00 and 14:00 hours, during which we could fly missions, but the distance to Rovaniemi was too great and I decided to go by car.

The meeting didn't end until just before eleven o'clock. I definitely didn't want to spend the entire night in Rovaniemi, so I told my driver we would be heading back to Petsamo immediately. He agreed.

Rovaniemi is the capital city of the Finnish province of Lapland. From there the so-called Polar Sea Road led north to the port city of Kirkenes. Several kilometers from Kirkenes a small road branched off to Petsamo. The Polar Sea Road was the most important supply route for the German forces on the Polar Sea Front.

We made excellent progress in our Mercedes automobile. About half way to our destination, however, the engine suddenly began to sputter and soon afterwards quit completely. That was the worst thing that could have happened to us; we were stuck on the Polar Sea Road. It was too dark to carry out repairs. It was also bitterly cold, about minus thirty-five degrees.

During the day the Polar Sea Road was always busy with traffic, but at night there was almost none. I didn't think it was a good idea to just sit in the car and hope that a vehicle might possibly come by. The danger of frostbite in the severe cold was too great. I told my driver that we would simply start walking, at least then we would be moving.

There was a prevailing area of high pressure with a beautiful clear sky. The snow was dry and ice-cold; it crunched beneath our feet. This sound was the only thing we could hear. No dogs barked, there were no vehicle noises or general sounds of civilization. It was deathly quiet. The northern lights filled the sky, hanging down like red and yellow curtains. It was an impressive natural spectacle.

Our walking produced the desired warmth. After a while I saw a weak glow appear on the horizon. It had to be a vehicle coming towards us. We walked and walked, but the light got no closer. Finally we realized that it was a star low on the horizon, shining so brightly that we mistook it for a vehicle.

After we had been walking for about two hours, we suddenly smelled wood smoke. Soon afterwards we came to a small side road, which led to a cabin with lit windows. I opened the door, and we saw Finnish soldiers. It was a small military outpost. From our uniforms, they immediately realized that we were Germans.

I explained our situation to the Finns and asked if they had a telephone. I was able to contact Finnish and, by way of them, German authorities. I was even able to telephone the airfield at Petsamo. After the Finns told us at which kilometer of the Polar Sea Road we were, I was able to state our exact position. A car subsequently came and returned us to Petsamo.

I have never forgotten this somewhat involuntary experience. For a central European, the absolute silence, combined with the cold and the Northern Lights, was extraordinary. Who comes up with the crazy idea of heading out onto the Polar Sea Road at night in such cold temperatures? Of course, it never would have happened if our car hadn't failed us."

On 1 March 1944 Günther Scholz was promoted to the rank of *Oberstleutnant*, with a seniority date of 1 May 1944. Coincident with the promotion, he was officially named *Kommodore* of JG 5.

"One day the telephone rang. I picked up and found myself speaking to *Oberst* von Cramon, who introduced himself as the chief-of-staff of the Commanding General of the German Air Force in Finland. He told me he had a mission for me. I was to do my best to sever the Murmansk railway. To this end I was to take part of my *Geschwader* to Alakurtti in central Finland. He also placed a *Staffel* of Ju 87 Stukas under my command for the task. Then our conversation ended.

I subsequently moved to Alakurtti with my *Stab* and elements of the II. *Gruppe*. How was I to carry out my mission? How was I to inflict lasting destruction on the Murmansk railway? That was no simple task. The railway consisted of a single track. From a height of 1,000 meters it was no more than a narrow stripe. Simply attacking the line made no sense, a station offered much better prospects. I had procured several maps from the senior staff so that I could better orientate myself.

The first thing, however, was to determine where the airfields used by the Russian fighters were located. And so we carried out a number of reconnaissance flights. In the course of these we also discovered several more dummy airfields, which required several low passes to identify them as such.

Once we knew where the Russians had their airfields, we could firm up our plans. We looked for a suitable railway station for our attacks. The most important criterion was the distance between the target and Alakurtti, thus the selection was not very great. I can no longer remember the name of the station.

We conducted the attack with several Stukas escorted by a number of our fighters. The weather was excellent. When we arrived over the chosen station, we found that luck was with us. At each station the single-track Murmansk railway split into several tracks. When we approached the station we saw that there was a train on the track heading north, while there was another train on the sidetrack.

The Stukas dropped their bombs on the station buildings and also tried to hit the tracks. The locomotives were strafed in an attempt to set them afire. We fighters also took part in that part of the attack. The damage was considerable, and this was confirmed by a subsequent reconnaissance flight.

During the night the Russians tried to repair the damage and fix the break in the Murmansk Railway as quickly as possible. We therefore repeated the attack the next day.

This process went on for about a week. The distance to the target area was considerable. Now and then there were engagements with enemy aircraft during the flight to or from the target. Most of our fighters had to remain with the Stukas, and because of the duration of the mission the others had little fuel for dogfighting. Staying with the Stukas during such a long flight was no easy task, as the Me had a much higher cruising speed. On reaching the target, the Stukas dove on their targets and then flew home at low level.

Then the weather changed, bringing rain and fog, and we halted our attacks. Our action had been a success, in that the Murmansk Railway had been severed at that spot for almost a week, and no more trains could pass.

When the weather prevented us from continuing our attacks and the Russians were able to work all day, they repaired everything with amazing speed. The bomb craters were filled in, new track was laid, the buildings were repaired, and the burnt locomotives and rail cars removed. The break in the Murmansk Railway had been eliminated.

During the war our efforts against the Murmansk Railway, that vital Soviet artery, always produced only short-lived results. Conscious of the importance of this supply route, the Russians mobilized all their forces to keep it alive.

My time in Alakurtti was not yet over. We were directed to support the army units stationed in that area. Central Finland is a country with very many lakes. The Soviets had emplaced a large number of artillery batteries along the thinly-manned German front and these repeatedly bombarded our positions. We were ordered to find out where these batteries were as a prelude to low-level attacks. Once again our efforts were aided by the Stukas, for which we were to provide fighter escort.

One day shells suddenly began falling on our airfield. Immediately there was great commotion and we feared that our aircraft might be hit. We had parked them around the perimeter of the airfield, which, fortunately for us, was very large. The Russians fired intermittently and from a great distance. I gave the order to get the aircraft into the air, away from the airfield. Our fighters took off very quickly, the Stukas took a bit longer. When all the aircraft were in the air, the firing stopped.

I was certain that the Russians would continue to harass us with their artillery. They would surely use it, now that they had discovered our airfield and were within range. I therefore ordered that, if we came under fire again, several fighters were to take off immediately and look for muzzle flashes. To no one's surprise, the next day the Russians repeated their little game. One of our pilots was able to make out the battery's position. We immediately expressed our gratitude with a concentrated attack on the Russian guns. We came in low and strafed them with our machine-guns. I don't know if we inflicted much damage, but there were no more attacks on our airfield.

I assume that the Russians had an observer sitting nearby, probably in a tree, from where he directed their fire. There is no other way that they could have pinpointed the airfield so well. The shells left large holes behind, but these were easily filled. Thank God that nothing happened to our aircraft or people."

One of JG 5's pilots who was particularly successful during the Alakurtti period was Theodor Weißenberger.

Born in 1914, Weißenberger was an enthusiastic glider pilot even before he joined the Luftwaffe. On 1 September 1941 he joined 1.(Z)/JG 77 in northern Norway as a *Feldwebel* and on 24 October scored his first victory. He shot down a total of twenty-three enemy machines as a *Zerstörer* pilot. In recognition of his success, *Oberfeldwebel* Weißenberger was awarded the German Cross in Gold on 6 September 1942.

Weißenberger was transferred to 6./JG 5 on 10 September 1942 and there began his rapid rise as a single-engined fighter pilot. On 13 November 1942, after his 38th victory, *Leutnant* Weißenberger was decorated with the Knight's Cross. *Feldwebel* Heinrich Bartels received the prestigious decoration the same day.

Multiple victories were a hallmark of Weißenberger's success as a fighter pilot, and his total rose rapidly. He shot down thirty-three enemy aircraft in March 1943 alone. On 1 June 1943 Weißenberger was promoted to *Oberleutnant* and soon afterwards, on 15 June, was placed in command of 7./JG 5. He surpassed the 100 victory mark on 4 July 1943 and on 2 August he and Heinrich Ehrler were awarded the Knight's Cross with Oak Leaves.

In September 1943 Weißenberger took over 6./JG 5 as *Kapitän*. After his 150th victory, at the end of March 1944 he was given command of the II. *Gruppe* of *Jagdgeschwader* 5. On 1 June 1944 the successful former *Zerstörer* pilot was promoted to *Hauptmann*. A few days later Weißenberger left the far northern theater and took over I./JG 5 as *Kommandeur*. Operating over the invasion front, in several weeks he recorded another twenty-five victories, all over fighter aircraft flown by western pilots. On 25 July 1944 he achieved his 200th victory.

Weißenberger subsequently trained on the Me 262 jet fighter and in November 1944 took over I./JG 7. After his promotion to *Major* on 1 January 1945, he led the *Geschwader* as *Kommodore* until the end of the war. Weißenberger scored eight more victories flying the Me 262 in the Defense of the Reich.

At the end of January 1945 Theodor Weißenberger was recommended for the Knight's Cross with Swords for his 200 victories, including twenty-three as a *Zerstörer* pilot and twenty-five over the invasion front. The recommendation was turned down, however, on the grounds that his number of victories was insufficient!!

A few years after the war, on 10 June 1950, Theodor Weißenberger was killed during an auto race at the Nürburgring speedway.

11
Fliegerführer

Günther Scholz's period as *Geschwaderkommodore* ended unexpectedly at the beginning of May 1944, when he was named *Jagdfliegerführer Norwegen*. The post had been created from the *Stab* of *Zerstörergeschwader* 76 in June 1944 and was directly subordinate to *Luftflotte* 5. The first *Jagdfliegerführer* Norwegen was *Oberstleutnant* Walter Grabmann, the *Kommodore* of ZG 76, who had been awarded the Knight's Cross on 14 September 1940 in recognition of his *Geschwader's* success.

Grabmann was succeeded by *Oberst* Carl-August Schumacher at the beginning of August 1941. He also wore the Knight's Cross, having received the decoration as *Kommodore* of JG 1 on 21 July 1940. After Schumacher was promoted to *Generalmajor* on 1 January 1944, he was in turn succeeded by *Oberstleutnant* Günther Scholz.

"My new post was in Stavanger. My command was limited to several elements of JG 5, based on the coast of Norway, and a signals regiment, which was also scattered in various locations along the Norwegian coast. From north to south, they monitored the airspace with their radars, for example the Freya type. The area for which I was responsible, however, extended only as far as abeam Trondheim and did not include northern Norway.

When I was named *Jagdfliegerführer* the commander of *Luftflotte* 5 was *General der Flieger* Josef Kammhuber, who had succeeded *Generaloberst* Hans-Jürgen Stumpff at the end of November 1943. Kammhuber came from the night-fighters and was a specialist in large radar installations. Near Stavanger he had had a radar control center built into a mountain. When I took over the position of *Jagdflieg-erführer Norwegen* this control center was handed over to me.

Kammhuber came to Stavanger for this occasion. He briefed me on my new duties, explained how the radar sets worked and how operations were controlled from my control center. We walked back and forth across a large meadow as we talked. Afterwards we looked for four-leaf clovers to unwind. For anyone who was watching, this must have been an unusual sight, after all Kammhuber was a *General der Flieger* and I an *Oberstleutnant*. I came to know Kammhuber as an extremely affable man. He was also a superior with whom one could speak about private matters."

Josef Kammhuber was born in 1896. As a volunteer, he experienced the hell of trench warfare on the Western Front in the First World War and rose to the rank of *Leutnant*. Kammhuber remained in the *Reichswehr* after the end of the war and trained as a pilot. After serving as a group leader in the Organizational Department of the *Reichsluftfahrministerium, in 1936 *Major* Kammhuber took command of a *Jagdgruppe*. (*State Aviation Ministry) He was subsequently promoted to *Oberst* and returned to the ministry as head of the Organizational Department.**

When war broke out in 1939, Kammhuber was chief-of-staff of *Luftflotte* 2 and at the beginning of 1940 he became the *Kommodore* of *Kampfgeschwader* 51. He subsequently led his *Geschwader* through the Western Campaign. Forced down behind enemy lines on 3 June 1940, Kammhuber was held by the French as a prisoner of war for a short time. He was later freed by advancing German forces.

Josef Kammhuber was then tasked with the formation of the 1. *Nachtjagddivision* and on 16 October 1940 was promoted to *Generalmajor*. In the years that followed, as *General der Nachtjagd* Kammhuber played a major role in the expansion and command of the German night-fighter force, and on 9 July 1941 he was awarded the Knight's Cross.

After the heavy defeats suffered by the night-fighter force in 1943, in the autumn of that year the air defense was reorganized and Josef Kammhuber, who by then had been promoted to *General der Flieger*, was relieved of his duties. He was sent to Norway, where he succeeded Hans-Jürgen Stumpff as commander of *Luftflotte* 5.

Shunted to a secondary theater of war by the Luftwaffe command, Kammhuber brought his experience, in particular his knowledge of radar, to Norway. For example, he had the previously-mentioned radar control center built in Stavanger.

"The interior of this control center reminded me of an ancient amphitheater. There were several rows of seats, one above the other. In the center was a huge wall, on which lights indicated the positions of our units and the enemy aircraft. One had this huge responsibility as fighter commander. If enemy units were reported approaching, I had to alert and commit the appropriate *Gruppe*.

My predecessor as *Jafü Norwegen*, whom I never met personally, had been an older man. Truth be told, among fighter pilots at that time I was one of the older men too. Most fighter pilots were in their early twenties, I was already thirty-three years old. My predecessor Schumacher had been in his late forties. His staff also consisted of older reserve officers.

I soon realized that the primary concern of these older gentlemen was procuring good food. They were more interested in their personal well-being than in attending to their duties. I therefore tried to somehow push these people out and transfer them to other positions. At the same time I brought in people I knew from JG 5 to serve in my staff, such as the technical officer, *Hauptmann* Probst, and *Stabsintendant* Berkefeld.

Stavanger had two airfields, Stavanger-Sola and Stavanger-Forus. The radar control center was near Sola. Most of the personnel were quartered in nearby private homes that had been requisitioned. Some of my staff and I also lived near the radar control center, in a lovely villa with a magnificent view.

It was summer 1944. Thousands of German soldiers were dying every day on the Russian Front. We were little affected by this murderous fighting, but I had never requested the position."

"When the first news of the events of 20th July 1944 reached us, we did not yet know what had happened and what the outcome was. We only heard that Hitler was dead. Our first thoughts were about the possibility of a peace agreement. We were not exactly enthusiastic about continuing the war no matter what the cost. In June the Allies had landed in France. The fronts in the east were equally shaky. Anyone with the slightest imagination could picture what the rest of the war would be like.

Subsequent information revealed to us in Norway the true facts of the events in Rastenburg and Berlin. Hitler was alive.

The assassination attempt against Hitler resulted in the creation of the position of National-Socialist leadership officer. I wanted to keep them from sending us any of these party soldiers, and my staff and I discussed the matter at length. We decided that someone should volunteer to take over the position, pro forma at least. Finally the technical officer, *Hauptmann* Bernhard Probst, volunteered. I then reported that he had become the so-called NSFO, and so for us the matter was settled."

In the autumn of 1944 the collapse of the German front in Russia began making itself felt in the far north. Germany's ally Finland had been forced to evacuate the occupied Soviet territories and was itself coming under fierce pressure. This resulted in a change of sides on the part of the Finns. On 19 September 1944 Finland concluded a separate peace treaty with the Soviet Union which obligated it to use military force to evict German forces from its territory. The Germans were given fourteen days to leave Finland. This deadline was impossible to meet, and after it expired there was fighting between the former allies which lasted until early 1945.

The Luftwaffe command took its first steps in response to the changed situation in mid-September 1944. On 15 September the headquarters of *Luftflotte* 5 was disbanded and was reorganized as the headquarters of the commanding general of the German Air Force in Norway. The headquarters was based in Oslo. Its first commanding general was *General der Flieger* Josef Kammhuber, the former commander of *Luftflotte* 5. On 10 October 1944 he handed command over to *Generalmajor* Ernst-August Roth in order to take on new duties.

As a result of the events in Finland, at the end of 1944 the elements of JG 5 still there returned to Norway, where they were stationed at various airfields along the Norwegian coast.

When Günther Scholz left JG 5, Heinrich Ehrler had succeeded him as *Geschwader* commander, just as he had followed him as *Kommandeur* of III./JG 5 about a year earlier. On 12 November 1944 an event took place which would have serious consequences for Heinrich Ehrler.

On 15 September 1944 Lancaster bombers of the Royal Air Force attacked the battleship "Tirpitz" in Alta Fjord in northern Norway and seriously damaged her. The British had attacked the "Tirpitz" a number of times, without, however, achieving the desired success. After the attack of 15 September 1944, the "Tirpitz" was moved south to Tromsö Fjord under the strictest secrecy. Because of the damage inflicted by the British bombing, the ship was no longer seaworthy and could only serve as a floating coastal battery. This secrecy was later to prove its undoing. As well, the battleship was not as well protected at its new location as it had been in the Alta Fjord.

At the beginning of November 1944 Heinrich Ehrler and his headquarters of JG 5 were based at Banak. On 9 November he received orders to fly to Bardufoss, several hundred kilometers to the southwest. Elements of the *Geschwader* were supposed to be reequipped and reorganized there. Ehrler was to make the necessary preparations and return to Banak on 11 November. For organizational reasons related to the reequipping, Ehrler postponed his return flight until 12 November 1944.

On that day the British carried out another raid against the "Tirpitz". Unlike the Luftwaffe, the British knew where the "Tirpitz" was tied up. On the German side, as the bombers approached there was a sequence of devastating errors in transmitting the air situation picture to the corresponding command posts.

At Bardufoss, 9./JG 5 was at three-minute readiness to protect the base from surprise attack. Just as *Major* Ehrler was about to begin his return flight to Banak, a report transmitted from the "Tirpitz" was received in the command post; but the ship only reported the sound of aircraft from an unknown direction and height.

Ehrler subsequently ordered the 9. *Staffel* to cockpit readiness and tried to obtain a more precise picture of the situation. A few minutes later, however, a second report of aircraft noises was received. Ehrler gave the order to scramble. He and his wingman were the first to take off. The 9. *Staffel*, which was supposed to follow him, was delayed by several minutes. While Ehrler was circling over the airfield, he found that his radio was not working. He was therefore unable to communicate with his aircraft or the fighter control officer.

On that day Heinrich Ehrler's victory total stood at 199. Because of the uncertain situation, he decided to set off alone with his wingman to perhaps intercept the enemy formation and shoot down his 200th.

The *Kommodore* of JG 5 did not know the exact location of the "Tirpitz", he only knew that the ship was somewhere in the Tromsö area. And so he flew in that direction at high altitude. When he reached the islands northeast of Tromsö, Ehrler continued flying west along the outer coast. He subsequently turned southeast and then headed in the direction of Balsfjord. He saw neither the "Tirpitz" nor the enemy aircraft. Ehrler therefore decided to return to his airfield at Alta.

During the flight he noticed a rising smoke column and flak bursts in the distance. The "Tirpitz" had just fallen victim to the attacking Lancaster formation. 1,204 members of the battleship's crew lost their lives.

A few days later, on 20 November 1944, Heinrich Ehrler scored his 200th victory. He had already been put up for the Knight's Cross with Diamonds, but it was not to be. A scapegoat was needed for the loss of the "Tirpitz".

Even if the 9. *Staffel* of his *Geschwader* had taken off with Ehrler, there is no way they could have reached the "Tirpitz" in time. Precious time had been lost in the confused command structure of the radar control centers. What doomed the battleship, however, was the cloak of secrecy surrounding its precise location, which was kept from the Luftwaffe posts which were supposed to protect it.

The *Kommodore* of JG 5 was accused of dereliction of duty for having taken off alone instead of directing the interception of the incoming bombers from his command post. Heinrich Ehrler was brought before a court martial for these alleged failures of command. Evidence which proved him innocent was ignored, and Heinrich Ehrler was sentenced to three years and two months imprisonment. Furthermore, he was demoted from a *Major* to a simple soldier, with the loss of all orders and decorations. This of course negated the recommendation for the Swords.

In January 1945 Ehrler's sentence was amended. It was commuted to three months in order to give the victor in 200 air battles the opportunity to redeem himself at the front!! The loss of rank was also lifted.

Günther Scholz followed the events surrounding his successor from a distance. Had he had still been in command of JG 5, he might have had to answer for the sinking of the German battleship.

"All that I heard personally was that Ehrler had been relieved, and it wasn't until later that I learned the exact reasons why. And apparently because they couldn't find anyone else, in addition to my post of *Jagdfliegerführer* I was also tasked with commanding the *Geschwader*. To be completely honest, I didn't take the matter very seriously. In my eyes the war was lost.

I had my own ideas about the affair. For reasons of secrecy, we had not been told about the transfer of the Tirpitz to Tromsö Fjord. The *Geschwader* also knew nothing about it. That's why it became such a failure for us. We had absolutely no idea what the English were up to. What was the reason for such an incursion? In my radar control center I heard not a word about the raid. I later learned why. The command structure in Norway was divided. My sector extended from Trondheim down to southern Norway. Why this was so, I do not know. Because of it, we didn't learn about the tragedy until it was already too late."

After his unjust trial, Heinrich Ehrler was a broken man. After he was ordered to redeem himself at the front, *Major* Theodor Weißenberger, a friend from their time together in JG 5, brought Ehrler to JG 7, where he arrived on 27 February 1945.

Heinrich Ehrler converted onto the Me 262 jet fighter and on 21 March 1945 shot down his first enemy aircraft in the Defense of the Reich. Ehrler took off on his last combat mission on 4 April. After shooting down two twin-engined bombers, he radioed his friend Theo Weißenberger and advised him that he was out of ammunition and was going to ram the nearest bomber. Then he said goodbye with the words, "See you again in Valhalla". Ehrler failed to

return from this sortic, however it is unclear whether he in fact rammed a third bomber. Ehrler scored a total of eight victories whilst flying the Me 262.

In addition to Heinrich Ehrler and Theodor Weißenberger, JG 5 had another pilot who surpassed the 200 victory mark. He was Walter Schuck. During the war a total of fifteen German fighter pilots recorded more than 200 victories.

Walter Schuck, born on 30 July 1920, scored his first victory on 15 May 1942. At that point he was an *Unteroffizier* attached to 7./JG 5. By April 1943 he had raised his victory total to thirty-four, and by autumn 1943 to more than sixty. Following his eighty-forth victory, on 8 April 1944 *Oberfeldwebel* Schuck was awarded the Knight's Cross while serving with 9./JG 5.

Walter Schuck scored his 100th victory on 15 June 1944. Two days later he shot down twelve enemy aircraft in a twenty-four hour period, and on 23 August his 150th victim fell from the sky. On 30 September 1944, after promotion to *Leutnant*, Schuck was decorated with the Knight's Cross with Oak Leaves. Then in November 1944 he was promoted to *Oberleutnant*.

Just like Heinrich Ehrler, Theodor Weißenberger also brought Walter Schuck to JG 7 in the spring of 1945. By that time Schuck had 198 victories to his credit. He added eight more victories while flying the Me 262, including four during a single pass through an American bomber stream on 10 April 1945. Later in the same flight, Schuck was himself hit and forced to bale out. The injuries he sustained kept him out of action for the rest of the war.

Back to February 1945, when the horror of the war caught up with Günther Scholz in peaceful Stavanger.

"In mid-February 1945 I suffered a personal tragedy. I received three telegrams almost simultaneously, one from my wife, then one from a Luftwaffe post and one from a district administrator. They told me that my parents had been killed in a terror raid on Magdeburg on 15 February 1945.

I was my parents' only son. They were still living in the firefighting school in Magdeburg-Heyrothsberge that my father had converted into an apartment house. And it was over that suburb of Magdeburg that numerous bombs had been dropped. I later learned that my parents' house had been struck by an aerial mine. The occupants of the house were in the unreinforced cellar, which had been designated a so-called air-raid cellar. The shock wave from the exploding aerial mine burst the lungs of those inside. The only survivor was my parents' long-haired Dachshund, which had probably been sheltered from the blast by my mother's upper body bending over it.

On receipt of the news I was immediately given fourteen days of so-called bombing leave, which by then was only granted when someone lost family members in a bombing raid. Previously it was given when a house or apartment was damaged by bombing. The scale of the enemy's bombing campaign ended this practice, after all, everyone couldn't go on leave.

I flew to Germany and first went to see my wife in Chemnitz, then we took the train to Magdeburg together. By then even this journey had become an adventure, and it took almost all day. The train halted repeatedly, once at Riesa Station. Everyone had to get off, as a large formation of American bombers had been reported heading our way. The passengers, including my wife and me, took cover in slit trenches on the station grounds.

I looked up and saw the bomber formation, or to be more precise the condensation trails, a huge number of condensation trails. In Riesa there was a steel mill not far from the station. I thought to myself that if that was the bombers' target, things could get hot, because we were within the target zone. I kept staring into the sky, but the bombers continued on in the direction of Berlin. We were very happy about that.

After some time we were told to get back on the train. The journey continued until the next interruption. One cannot imagine the conditions that prevailed at that time.

After arriving in Magdeburg-Heyrothsberge, I stood for a short time before my parents' house. Half of it was gone, collapsed by the blast wave from the aerial mine. My parents' apartment was also badly damaged. Some of the wrecked furniture lay below on the ground floor. My wife and I looked to see what was salvageable. We retrieved several valuable carpets from the apartment along with bedding, a pair of shoes and some personal things, whatever we could find. We collected everything in the yard. My father's car, an Opel, was there too. I had also left my Hansa sports car with my parents. Both vehicles were undamaged. We decided to drive both back to Chemnitz.

I first had to procure gasoline for the trip, and my sports car had no battery. I went to the district administrator for permission to fuel the vehicles and drive them to Chemnitz. My rank certainly helped, however I could only obtain enough gasoline for one vehicle, and I was also unable to get a car battery. I filled the tank of my father's Opel and we loaded the two cars with my parents' surviving possessions. Then I hooked the Hansa to the Opel. With the sports car with no battery in tow and my wife at the wheel, we set off for Chemnitz.

We drove down the autobahn at a slow pace. The Opel had a radio. After some time a report was broadcast that low-flying aircraft were approaching along the autobahn. These warnings were still broadcast at that time and the information was very accurate. I thought to myself, it would be good to make it to the next bridge. Luckily there were many on that section of road. We made it, stopped, and waited. Less than ten minutes later a pair of American fighters came roaring towards us, shooting at anything that moved. They couldn't see us under the bridge and thus couldn't hit us. After that we decided to avoid the autobahn as much as possible.

Then our rope broke. As the Hansa had no battery, neither the windshield wipers nor the horn were working. Consequently my wife was unable to alert me, and there was no point in crying out. While I kept looking in the mirrors at short intervals, by the time I realized that my wife wasn't behind me I was already some distance away. I turned around, reconnected my wife's car, and we continued our difficult journey.

It was already late at night when we approached Chemnitz. From many kilometers away we could see the sky turning red. I knew exactly what that meant, the city was on fire.

My in-law's house was on the outskirts. When we arrived there we found a crowd of about thirty people. They were all acquaintances or friends of the family who had lost everything during the night. It wasn't until the next day that the scale of the attack of 5 March 1945 became evident. The old Chemnitz was no more.

It was now time for me to return to Norway. I took the train to Berlin, and this trip also took a very long time. In the capital I reported to the responsible post, and after several telephone calls I was directed to a Ju 88 that had just come out of a repair facility and was supposed to fly back to Norway. In this way I returned to my post in Stavanger by the fastest means possible.

Since *Major* Ehrler's dismissal, I had been acting both as *Fliegerführer* and commander of the remaining elements of JG 5, and now both staffs were officially combined.

I remained in Stavanger until the end of the war. I ceased operational flying after being named *Jagdfliegerführer*. The airfield was at least fifteen minutes from my office. I spent most of my time with my staff, which in any case was about the size of a brigade staff, in the radar control center. There wasn't much to do. If incursions were reported, I controlled the missions. Aerial activity was much less than in the south in the Defense of the Reich.

During the final weeks of the war, a rumor suddenly began that Norway was to be declared a fortress. The units based in Norway were ordered to practice handling weapons. The members of my staff were mostly technicians and mechanics. At some point in their training they had been taught to shoot, but no more.

And so we set up a firing range in Stavanger and practiced firing pistols, rifles and machine-guns. We prepared for the defense of Norway."

"Then, suddenly, fifteen to twenty German aircraft flew over the Baltic and southern Sweden to Norway from the Courland Pocket. Every possible type was represented, including several Fw 190s and Me 109s. Many had brought their first and even second mechanics with them. How they managed this remained a mystery to us.

The flow of rations to Norway also increased. Whole boatloads of preserves, for example, were delivered to the country. All of this was part of preparations to defend the country as a fortress. We asked ourselves, what was the point? We couldn't defend Norway alone, it wouldn't work. What were they thinking?

With the war in its final stages in Berlin, the order was cancelled. Norway was not to be defended to the last man after all.

The preserves that were delivered to the country later stood us in good stead, however. We had stored them in the buildings around Stavanger-Sola airfield.

A few hours before the German forces in Norway surrendered, the commanding general ordered me to Oslo one last time. In Germany the war was already over. I boarded my Me 108 and reported to the Holmenkollen, where the Luftwaffe headquarters was situated.

There were many other officers there, and we were issued final instructions for the imminent surrender. The most important thing was to burn all documents, including personal papers. Nothing in writing was to be allowed to all into English hands. Afterwards I bade farewell to the commanding general. Ernst-August Roth had been promoted to *Generalleutnant* on 1 January 1945.

At dusk I flew from Oslo back to Stavanger. There were fires everywhere. As ordered, the units and posts were burning all their documents. After I landed I gave the order to do the same. The war was over."

12
Homecoming and New Beginning

"After the surrender we were initially housed on the Stavanger-Sola airfield. Later we were sent from there to an internment camp for former members of the Luftwaffe at Boemoen near Bergen. As I was the senior serving officer, I was named camp commander. In the camp there were about 500 women and 1,500 soldiers. We were under an English command based in Bergen.

When word came that we were to be moved to this so-called reservation camp, *Stabsintendant* Berkefeld, my former IVa*, came up with the idea of taking with us some of the preserves stored on the airfield at Sola. (*Chief Administrative Officer) The English treated us quite humanely, and we were able to move about freely within the camp. We were also permitted to take our personal possessions with us. In this way we were able to take along some of the preserves.

When we arrived at the Boemoen, unnoticed by the English we built a double wall in one of the large camp barracks. Several boards were removed from the new wall to gain access and then nailed back up again. Anyone who didn't know would never suspect that behind the wall of the barracks' inner room there was another room and then the outer wall. It was there that we hid our preserves.

The genius of Berkefeld's idea soon became apparent. We continued to be treated well by the English, however our rations were poor and usually consisted of rolled oats, rice or corn. Happily, we were now in the situation of being able to supplement our meager diet with several tins of meat.

As commander of the Boemoen camp, I was often summoned to the British post responsible for us. Despite having lost the war, we kept our pride. On my first meeting with my English counterpart I discovered that he spoke good German. I also understood some English. We could thus have communicated directly with one another quite well. But no, each of us had brought an interpreter. Mine was a German *Oberfeldwebel.*

First the English drove me to the Stavanger airfields of Sola and Forus. We inspected the aircraft hangars, the repair facility and all of the other buildings that were part of the airfield. Our aircraft were still there and the personal that flew and maintained them were in the internment camp.

Curiously the English were not at all interested in the Me 109 or the Fw 190, which were all scrapped in Norway. They were more interested in the He 111, the Ju 88 and even the Ju 52.

The first inmates were shipped out of the internment camp in July 1945. By then the Luftwaffe personnel in the Boemoen camp had been joined by members of the army and navy. Eventually they were taken to Bergen or Stavanger. Transport ships were gathered in the ports of southern Norway to take the German soldiers back to their homeland.

Soon, however, a rumor reached us that the English had handed many of the returnees over to the French. The ships had left Norway, supposedly bound for Lübeck or Hamburg, but soon afterwards they changed course and sailed to France. It was the purest form of slave trading. Many who had thought they were going home ended up working in French coal mines under extremely difficult conditions. Many lost their lives, in part through hunger.

They had begun by shipping out the lower ranks. The so-called camp command, consisting mostly of older officers, was to follow later.

Roughly in August 1945, we pilots were asked if we would ferry aircraft to Germany. The English had collected a number of He 111s, Ju 88s and Ju 52s, and they wanted to move them to Germany. They sought out the most experienced pilots possible for the task.

By that time the number of personnel in the Boemoen camp had shrunk significantly. I saw in the question an opportunity to go home. I had never flown a He 111 or a Ju 88, but I could fly a Ju 52. So I volunteered. *Major* Treppe, a former member of my *Jagdfliegerführer* staff, volunteered to be my copilot. Together we were given the task of ferrying a Ju 52 from Stavanger to Lübeck.

The aircraft was packed with sick German soldiers and pregnant Norwegian women. The English were eager to be rid of both groups. The Norwegian girls were pregnant with the children of German soldiers and some had married them. The end of the war brought the collapse of their world, for they also lost their homeland. Suddenly their own countrymen wanted nothing more to do with them. The scenes that were played out there are indescribable.

Major Treppe and I boarded the Ju. No English accompanied us on the flight. We made a fuel stop in Copenhagen. We were treated very generously. While the sick and the pregnant women were looked after and the aircraft refueled, we were permitted to go into the barracks on the airfield where the English had set up their mess hall. The place was filled with the wonderful smell of tea. They served it to us with milk, and it tasted wonderful. It had been a long time since I had drunk such excellent tea.

Afterwards we flew on to Lübeck, where we handed over the Ju 52. The sick and the pregnant were taken to hospital and cared for. The pilots who had flown the aircraft from Norway were put in a truck and driven to an old schoolhouse, where the English again took charge of us. We were not released.

We spent the next few weeks wandering around and literally killing time. We were permitted to leave the building and go into Lübeck. One could have kept on going, but if one had been picked up without papers, things would definitely have been much worse. So we waited for our release and the production of the necessary documents. For me this period ended on 28 November 1945.

We were put in trucks for the last time. My designated release point was Herfurth, where my father's brother lived with his family. I couldn't go straight to Chemnitz to my wife, because for the present no one was being released into the Soviet zone.

It was already dark when we drove through Herfurth. Up front in the cab of the truck sat two Englishmen. I got their attention and the truck stopped. I took my small case with my few remaining possessions and got out. The truck drove away. My days as a prisoner of war were over.

In the dark night I asked my way to Veilchenstraße and found the house of my uncle's family. At least I had a roof over my head for the time being, and in the days that followed I was able to think about what I should do. My most urgent desire was to make contact with Chemnitz. I had been out of contact with my wife since the beginning of March 1945, and she had no idea as to my fate during the last six months. Telephoning was not possible. From Herfurth there was no direct line to Chemnitz. And so I wrote a letter.

I waited impatiently and the days passed, then I received a reply from my wife. She wrote to me that she and her parents were still in Chemnitz and that she didn't want to leave the city. The factory had been destroyed, but the house and grounds were untouched. She wanted me to come to her.

I had begun planning for the future even before the war ended. When I was in Berlin in early March 1945 I had spoken about it to my friend Hans Schmoller-Haldy.

On 23 February 1942, not long after I was transferred out of JG 54, Schmoller-Haldy had been shot down by flak and suffered serious head injuries. After recovering, he did not return to the front. Instead he served on the staff of the *General der Jagdflieger* until the end of the war.

We two were connected by our time together in the Luftwaffe. During our conversation in Berlin, I spoke with him about what would happen if my wife and I, for whatever reasons, were unable to live in Chemnitz after the war. Schmoller-Haldy replied that his parents owned a house in Munich and that I could temporarily occupy a room there. He lived there too.

I had mentioned this in the letter to my wife. If we didn't see each other again, she could find me in Munich. Now I had her reply in my hands. I didn't think about it for long and quickly made the decision to go to Chemnitz. The Russians wouldn't stay long and would surely leave soon.

I spent the next few weeks in the house of my uncle and celebrated Christmas with the family. I started on my way in February 1946. My cousin's husband was about my size and gave me civilian clothes. I had none. I was still wearing the remains of my uniform, with shoulder tabs and collar patches removed and the metal buttons replaced with others. That's how I had walked around Lübeck since my release. I didn't want to cross the border in my former service uniform, however, and so I accepted the civilian clothes, including a heavy coat, as it was cold. I replaced my small suitcase with a rucksack, after all I didn't have much to carry.

I took the train from Lübeck to the southern Harz near Nordhausen. The border then ran through the small town of Ellrich-Walkenried. Then it was still called the demarcation line. Only later did it become the fortified border between the two Germanys. On the way there I met four former members of the navy. We apparently had the same destination, so I joined them. The men were crewmen on minesweepers that had been commandeered by the British. They had been put to work on behalf of the Allies, clearing minefields from the harbor entrances laid by the Germans during the war. It was very dangerous work.

For some reason the English had given the four sailors a week's leave and they were on their way home. They still had on their navy uniforms, over which they were wearing overcoats they had procured somewhere. Thus attired, we approached the guarded demarcation line.

When we arrived, we stopped for a while and observed. We saw that every ten minutes two Russian sentries passed the point where we wanted to cross the border. That was sufficient time. Unnoticed, we slipped across into the Soviet zone and quickly moved on to the nearest village. We crawled into a shed and got some sleep before carrying on.

Afterwards we walked to the nearest station and together we took the train to Leipzig. There our paths parted. I travelled on to Chemnitz, where I got off at the main station. I walked through the wrecked city to the house of my in-laws. They weren't expecting me, how could they have? There had been no opportunity for me to let them know I was coming. I lobbed a few snowballs against a windowpane. Several faces appeared behind the glass, and when they saw me standing below their joy knew no bounds. At last I was able to hold my wife in my arms again. The war was thus finally over.

I had lost my parents and my home in Magdeburg. My wife and I took up residence in a room in my in-laws' house. Also living there was my wife's sister, whose husband was a prisoner in Russia.

My father-in-law's factory had been destroyed in the raid on Chemnitz on 5 March 1945. He had already begun starting over and had purchased a building in neighboring Neukirchen that had once been a shoe factory. The machinery that was still usable was brought from the city. Some of it had sustained serious fire damage and had to be repaired. I had once wanted to become an engineer. In order to be granted admittance to the technical academy in Hanover, one had to be able to show one year of practical experience. During this period I gained some insight into the mechanic's trade. Consequently, I boldly asserted to my father-in-law that I was a mechanic. In reality I knew little about the trade.

In this way I found my first employment in my father-in-law's factory. Together with a real mechanic, we gradually got the machines working again. We completely disassembled them. Parts that were broken or unusable were replaced. I very much enjoyed the filing and assembly, in short the entire job.

The factory began working again after about six months. Before the war it had produced the tickets for the state railroad, but now we were the only ones working for the local railroad. We began on this basis, and in the years that followed the business was built up little by little.

I of course received a salary, and together with my wife was able to stand on my own two feet. There was still a question with the rations cards, for I was not officially a resident. In the truest sense of the word I lived off my in-laws. My father-in-law was very resourceful. He knew the butcher and the baker, and he always managed to obtain enough to feed me too. This situation, of course, could not go on indefinitely. Personally, I wanted to report to the authorities.

My father-in-law went with me, and his contacts were helpful there too. We went straight to the apartment of the responsible party leader and my father-in-law introduced me. I concealed my true rank and identified myself as a *Hauptmann*. I stated that my parents were dead and their home destroyed. My wife was from Chemnitz and I wanted very much to live there. I obviously gained the man's sympathy. He was very kind to me and reported me to his party office. I then had to report to the police. I had officially arrived in Chemnitz and from that day forward I received my own rations cards.

For me it was the beginning of a new chapter in my life which was to be no less eventful."

APPENDICES

The Military Career of Günther Scholz
Born 8 December 1911 in Breslau
Entered the military on 8 April 1934

Promotions

15/06/1934	*Seekadett*
01/10/1934	*Obermatrose*
01/01/1935	*Oberstabsmatrose*
01/04/1935	*Fähnrich*
01/10/1935	*Oberfähnrich*
01/04/1936	*Leutnant*
01/10/1938	*Oberleutnant*
01/11/1941	*Hauptmann*
01/04/1943	*Major*
01/03/1044	*Oberstleutnant* (Seniority Date 01/05/1944)

Decorations

08/04/1938	Service Decoration Fourth Class
01/06/1939	Spanish Cross in Gold with Swords
01/06/1939	Spanish Medalla de Campagna
01/06/1939	Spanish Cruz de Guerra
17/09/1939	Iron Cross, Second Class
Dec. 1939	Commemorative Medal of 1 October 1938 (Sudetenland Medal)
Dec. 1939	Commemorative Medal of the Return of the Memel District
25/05/1940	Iron Cross, First Class
28/09/1940	Honor Goblet for Distinguished Achievements in the Air War
23/05/1941	Operational Flying Clasp for Fighters in Gold

01/09/1941	Wound Badge in Black
23/08/1942	Finnish Freedom Cross Third Class
08/09/1942	German Cross in Gold
02/12/1942	Operational Flying Clasp for Fighters with Pendant and Mission Number "400"

Deployments

08/04/1934 – 13/06/1934	6./II. S.S.O., Stralsund
14/06/1934 – 31/03/1935	Mürwick Naval School
01/04/1935 – 31/05/1935	II. S.S.O.. Stralsund
15/06/1935 – 31/10/1935	II. M.M.A., Wilhelmshaven
01/11/1935 – 14/04/1936	Salzwedel Flight Training School
15/04/1936 – 14/03/1937	I./JG 232, Bernburg
15/03/1937 – 14/02/1938	I./JG 135, Bad Aibling
15/02/1938 – 27/02/1938	10./JG 137, Bernburg
28/02/1938 – 10/09/1938	RLM Special Staff 10 (Spain)
11/09/1938 – 31/03/1939	I./JG 131, Jesau
01/11/1938 – 31/03/1939	I./JG 130, Jesau
01/04/1939 – 14/07/1939	I./JG 1, Jesau
15/07/1939 – 14/07/1940	*Kapitän* 1./JG 21
15/07/1940 – 10/02/1942	*Kapitän* 7./JG 54
11/02/1942 – 20/03/1942	*Kommandeur* IV./JG 1
21/03/1942 – 31/05/1943	*Kommandeur* III./JG 5
01/06/1943 – 29/02/1944	*Geschwaderführer* JG 5
01/03/1944 – 09/05/1944	*Kommodore* JG 5
10/05/1944 – 28/02/1945	*Jagdfliegerführer Norwegen*
29/02/1945 – 08/05/1945	*Jagdfliegerführer Norwegen* and *Kommodore* of JG 5

On the following pages the author has attempted to create a detailed list of the victories achieved by Günther Scholz. No logbooks or other such records were available to him. The author would be grateful for any additional information or possible corrections.

Number	Date	Rank	Unit
1	19/08/1938	*Leutnant*	3./J 88
2	13/05/1940	*Oberleutnant*	1./JG 21
3	20/05/1940	*Oberleutnant*	1./JG 21
4	26/05/1940	*Oberleutnant*	1./JG 21
5	26/05/1940	*Oberleutnant*	1./JG 21
6	25/08/1940	*Oberleutnant*	7./JG 54
7	28/08/1940	*Oberleutnant*	7./JG 54
8	02/09/1940	*Oberleutnant*	7./JG 54
9	28/09/1940	*Oberleutnant*	7./JG 54
10	23/06/1941	*Oberleutnant*	7./JG 54
11	30/06/1941	*Oberleutnant*	7./JG 54
12	30/06/1941	*Oberleutnant*	7./JG 54
13	30/06/1941	*Oberleutnant*	7./JG 54
14	06/07/1941	*Oberleutnant*	7./JG 54
15	06/07/1941	*Oberleutnant*	7./JG 54
16	07/07/1941	*Oberleutnant*	7./JG 54
17	07/07/1941	*Oberleutnant*	7./JG 54
18	10/07/1941	*Oberleutnant*	7./JG 54
19	12/07/1941	*Oberleutnant*	7./JG 54
20	14/07/1941	*Oberleutnant*	7./JG 54
21	21/07/1941	*Oberleutnant*	7./JG 54
22	01/08/1941	*Oberleutnant*	7./JG 54
23	19/09/1941	*Oberleutnant*	7./JG 54
24	26/09/1941	*Oberleutnant*	7./JG 54
25	30/09/1941	*Oberleutnant*	7./JG 54
26	04/10/1941	*Oberleutnant*	7./JG 54
27	11/10/1941	*Oberleutnant*	7./JG 54
28	28/04/942	*Hauptmann*	*Stab* III./JG 5
29	18/05/942	*Hauptmann*	*Stab* III./JG 5
30	14/07/942	*Hauptmann*	*Stab* III./JG 5
31	12/08/942	*Hauptmann*	*Stab* III./JG 5
32	05/03/943	*Hauptmann*	*Stab* III./JG 5
33			
34	18/08/943	*Major*	*Stab* JG 5

Location	Time	Type
west of Flix on the Ebro		Polikarpov I-16
east of Löwen, Belgium	06:40	Curtiss
west of Péronne, France	18:22	Morane 406
Lens-Douai area, France	09:06	Hawk-75A
Lens-Douai area, France	09:16	Hawk-75A
west of Folkestone, England	20:10	Spitfire
Canterbury area, England	17:20	Hurricane
Canterbury area, England	13:55	Spitfire
	11:07	Spitfire
north of Kaunas, Russia	11:50	Tupolev SB-2
Daugavpils area, Russia	12:10	Ilyushin DB-3
Daugavpils area, Russia	12:12	Ilyushin DB-3
Daugavpils area, Russia	12:14	Ilyushin DB-3
east of Ostrov, Russia	10:00	Tupolev SB-3
east of Ostrov, Russia	10:07	Tupolev SB-3
east of Ostrov, Russia	15:40	Tupolev SB-3
east of Ostrov, Russia	15:41	Tupolev SB-3
east of Pskov, Russia	09:15	Tupolev SB-3
	16:00	Ilyushin DB-3
	03:30	Polikarpov I-16
Vereteni, Russia	20:55	Tupolev SB-3
near Luga, Russia	19:05	Ilyushin DB-3
Leningrad area, Russia	14:00	Polikarpov I-153
	16:07	Polikarpov I-18
	15:40	Polikarpov I-153
	08:35	Polikarpov I-18
	11:10	Polikarpov I-26
		Hurricane
20 km west of Murmansk, Russia	10:25	Hurricane
Murmansk area, Russia	12:35	Hurricane
near Ura-Guba, Russia	14:30	MiG-1
	12:00	Ilyushin Il-2
west of Cape Korabelnye, Russia	16:24	Kittyhawk

PHOTO SECTION

Deutschlandflug 1933.

A Klemm training aircraft wearing the emblem of the German Air Sports Association (DLV).

A Heinkel Kadett

From 6 February until 31 March 1934, Günther Scholz (second from right) took part in another flight training course given by the DVL at Heyrothsberge near Magdeburg.

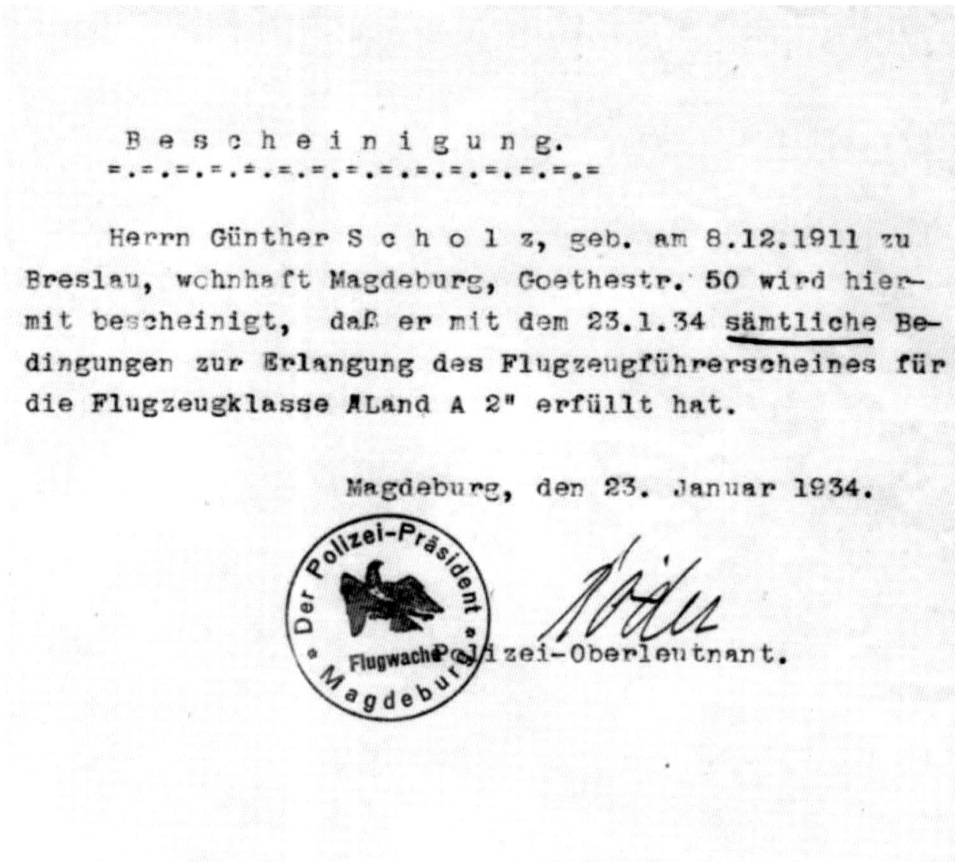

B e s c h e i n i g u n g.

=.=.=.=.=.=.=.=.=.=.=.=.=.=.=

Herrn Günther S c h o l z, geb. am 8.12.1911 zu Breslau, wohnhaft Magdeburg, Goethestr. 50 wird hiermit bescheinigt, daß er mit dem 23.1.34 sämtliche Bedingungen zur Erlangung des Flugzeugführerscheines für die Flugzeugklasse „Land A 2" erfüllt hat.

Magdeburg, den 23. Januar 1934.

Der Polizei-Präsident Flugwache Magdeburg

Polizei-Oberleutnant.

Certificate for successful participation in a pilot training course given by the German Air Sports Association

Deutsches Reich

Flugzeugführerschein

Nr. 87

für Herrn Günter Scholz

Oberpräsident der Provinz Sachsen
(Stempel der ausstellenden Behörde)

(Eigenhändige Unterschrift des Inhabers)

Magdeburg, den 5. Feb. 1934
(Ort)

Der Oberpräsident
Im Auftrage:

(Unterschrift)

Scholz's civilian pilot's license, issued on 5 February 1934 in Magdeburg.

Field exercises during basic training on Dänholm in June 1934.

The Korporal demonstrates how to dig a foxhole.

Return from Dänholm. Günther Scholz is on the left in the front row.

Classes in theory at the navy school in Mürwick.

Sailing lessons in the Flensburger Förde.

Kapitänleutnant Wilhelm Bloser, wearing his trademark white handkerchief with his navy uniform.

Firing pistols and machine-guns.

Scholz's mother during a visit to Mürwick.

Scholz in his dress uniform.

Led by its commander, Kapitänleutnant Wilhelm Bloser, the battalion from the Mürwick Naval School attracts everyone's attention as it marches through Dresden.

The battalion in Dresden. An arrow marks Günther Scholz's position in the upper photo.

Lunch in the "Little Italian Village" during the battalion's visit to Dresden.

laue Jungen auf dem Marsch durch Dresden / Hunderte zogen mit, Tausende sahen zu

Aufn. Koch

In der Seestadt, wo diese 180 Mann starke Marineabteilung, die am Donnerstag Dresdner Museen besuchte, stationiert ist, ist ihr Anblick etwas Alltägliches, Selbstverständliches. Es ist keine Sensation mehr, ähnlich wie am Morgen, wenn der charakteristische, langgezogene Ruf der Fischhändler „Goooold-bütt, Goooold-bütt, Goooold-bütt" Neugierige anlockt.

Anders bei uns! Hier im Binnenlande, wo es bestimmt mehr Balken als Wasser gibt, wurde ihr Marsch vom Hauptbahnhof durch die Innenstadt zu einem Ereignis, zu einem Triumphzug. Hunderte marschierten mit, Tausende sahen zu. Überall die erhobene Rechte, als sie vorbeikamen, Sinnbild der innigen Verbundenheit mit unserer stolzen kleinen Reichsmarine. Vorweg in treuer treuer Kameradschaft die Kapelle des I. (Jäger-) Btl. JR. 10, Obermusikmeister Thiele. Dann der „Besuch" unter Führung von Kapitänleutnant Bloser. Schneidige Kerle. Die ersten sechs Dreierreihen alles Zwei-Meter-Riesen, die wirklich nicht mehr auf einen Ausguck ihres Schiffes zu klettern brauchen. Weiße Mütze mit Band, darunter bronzebraune Gesichter, straff die Haltung, kühn und gesammelt der Blick. Winkende Hände von allen Seiten. Einem Exoten, schätzungsweise Südamerika, Parana oder Rio Negro, blieb der Mund offenstehen. Einem anderen ging sichtlich der Zigarillo aus, und er merkte es gar nicht. Eine typische englische Miß aus merry old England knurrte etwas, das wie ein widerstrebendes Kompliment klang.

Wacker hielten die Landeshauptstädter Schritt mit der Kolonne. Mancher gelangte im Eifer so ganz wo anders hin, als er ursprünglich beim Fortgehen aus seinem Büro beabsichtigte. Große Freude, als eine Frau unter den Seeleuten einen Bekannten entdeckt zu haben schien. Selig schaute ein kleiner blonder Fünfjähriger an der Hand seiner Mutti zu dem ungewohnten Blickfang herüber. Überhaupt gab es da viel „Blickfänger": einmal bei den Jan Maats in der blauen Uniform, die ganz geschickt mit den Augen funkten. Andererseits flog auch mancher bewundernde Gruß aus dunklen und hellen Augensternen zu den Reihen herüber.

Mit rührend hilflos vor der Brust gekreuzten Händen lehnte im Türrahmen ihres Geschäftes auf der Prager Straße ein junges Mädchen, leuchtenden Auges, und staunte. Ihr Herz stand in Flammen. Dichtbesetzte Fenster. Oft lugten viele von drin durch die Scheiben, so aus einem Kuchenladen heraus. Hoch auf Wagen hockten die Menschen. Aller Verkehr stockte. Auf der Leiter klopfte ein Fensterputzer mit der Hand den Takt zur Marschmusik. „Ja, soo is 's recht", murmelte ein altes Mütterchen. Und dem Eisgrauen um die Siebzig herum rollte es verdächtig-feucht unter der Brille hervor. Auf dem Altmarkt summte alles mit: „Dir woll'n wir treu ergeben sein". Noch gerade rechtzeitig geriet in der Schloßstraße ein eilig nach vorn stürmender sehnsüchtiger Kochlehrling mit hoher weißer Ballonmütze und wild geschwungenem Kochlöffel herzu, um „sein Teil mitzubekommen". Auch der erwerbslose Volksgenosse in einer Jacke aus braunem Velvetonstoff schob sein Kind schnell in Richtung Adolf-Hitler-Platz weiter, um nichts zu verpassen. Dort marschierte alles auf, rückte dann in die Museen ab. Ob es den „Marinern" dort gefallen hat? Sicher ebensogut wie tags zuvor auf der Bastei und dem Königstein. Abends sah man viele im Schauspielhaus. Am Sonntag geht es wieder gen Norden.

HLK.

A contemporary newspaper article about the sailors' visit to the capital of Saxony.

Günther Scholz stands guard at the navy school in February 1935.

In bivouac during the platoon leader's course at Stralsund in May 1935 (Günther Scholz on the far right).

Photo taken during a two-day battalion march in Stralsund. On the left is Fähnrich Günther Scholz.

Günther Scholz as a Korporal with the 1st Battery of the II Naval Artillery Battalion in Wilhelmshaven, 1935.

Major Rudolf Trautvetter, commander of the Salzwedel Flight Training School.

The officer cadets march to the flight line.

In the mess hall.

Hangars packed with training aircraft at Salzwedel.

Günther Scholz in the cockpit of an Ar 66 at Salzwedel.

Engine running, a He 51 just prior to takeoff.

He 51 A-1s of the 3. Staffel / Jagdgruppe Bernburg.

Flight during the Reich Party Congress of 1936.

Crash-landings.

Staffelkapitän Oberleutnant Hans-Heinrich Brustellin (left) and Leutnant Günther Scholz (center).

At the Bork gunnery range (Brustellin and Scholz).

Funeral ceremony at Bernburg after a fatal aircraft accident.

Bruno Loerzer wearing the Pour le Mérite and the Knight's Cross of the Iron Cross.

The airmen enter Bad Aibling.

Major Max Ibel, commander of the new Jagdgruppe.

Günther Scholz in civilian dress on the Predigstuhl near Bad Reichenhall.

Leutnant Hans Schmoller-Haldy.

Outing to the Walchensee. Günther Scholz with Karl Montag (left) and Dieter Hrabak (right). Born on 19 December 1914, Dietrich Hrabak served with Günther Scholz from the time he joined the navy in 1934 until Bad Aibling.

Hrabak was already a Gruppenkommandeur when the war broke out. He was shot down on his very first combat mission over Poland, the first Luftwaffe fighter pilot to meet such a fate.

He scored his first victory on 13 May 1940 and by October of the same year his score stood at sixteen. On 21 October 1940, Hauptmann Hrabak, Kommandeur of the II. Gruppe of Jagdgeschwader 54, was awarded the Knight's Cross.

During the war Hrabak rose to the rank of Oberstleutnant and commanded Jagdgeschwader 52 and 54. He scored a total of 125 victories, for which he was awarded the Knight's Cross with Oak Leaves (337th recipient).

Dietrich Hrabak and Günther Scholz.

The two photographs below show the young fighter pilots of the Jagdgruppe from Bad Aibling during a pleasant outing to the Tegernsee in the summer of 1937. Of these eight men, six rose to become Geschwaderkommodore during the war.

Left to right:

Hannes Trautloft (Kommodore, Jagdgeschwader 54)
Dietrich Hrabak (Kommodore Jagdgeschwader 52 and 54)
Karl Montag
Dr. Veit Vogel
Hans-Heinrich Brustellin (Kommodore, Jagdgeschwader 106)
Günther Scholz (Kommodore, Jagdgeschwader 5)
Wolfgang Schellmann (Kommodore, Jagdgeschwader 27)
Günther Radusch (Kommodore, Nachtjagdgeschwader 5, 2, 3)

Günther Scholz during a demonstration to members of the Hitler Youth at Prien am Chiemsee.

Günther Scholz with the 10. Staffel of the Jagdgruppe Bernburg in preparation for deployment to Spain.

Second from the left is Leutnant Wilhelm Ensslen, who later achieved much success in Spain.

Seat of the Nationalist government in Burgos.

Public maps show the progress of the war to date.

Oberleutnant Galland before the entrance to a villa, where the Staffel was quartered at La Cenia.

The train in which 3./J 88's personnel lived. Here Oberleutnant Galland is seen in the window of the mess car.

Twin-bed cabin in the sleeping car.

Washing up in the Rio Alcanadre near Sarinena.

A Red armored car, knocked out on the road to the front near Sarinena. On the right is interpreter Löffler.

Günther Scholz in front of a blooming cactus at the side of the road. Note their relative sizes.

With interpreter Löffler on the beach at Vinaroz.

The Nationalist cruiser "Todod por la patria" (Everything for the Fatherland) at Vinaroz.

Günther Scholz as duty officer in front of the Staffel quarters, a schoolhouse in La Cenia.

Pilots enjoying the sun between sorties. In the deck chair is Günther Scholz.

3./J 88's Staffel command post on the airfield at La Cenia.

Pilots of J 88.

His face still swollen, Scholz relaxes on the beach. From left: Leutnant Heinrich, Leutnant Scholz, Leutnant Losigkeit.

Hauptmann Gotthard Handrick, Kommandeur of J 88, in the W 34 en route to Tetuan.

Armorers and mechanics service the Kommandeur's aircraft (h = Hermann, Handrick's pseudonym).

Aircraft of 2./J 88, the so-called Top Hat Staffel.

Werner Mölders relieves Adolf Galland as commander of 3./J 88. Third from the left is Günther Scholz.

The Gruppe's officers celebrate Pentecost with champagne and wild get-ups; second from the left is Werner Mölders, fifth from the left Günther Scholz.

Günther Scholz and Fritz Losigkeit reading the Legion news.

The grave site of Leutnant Haupt, shot down on 2 June 1938. The inscription reads:

"Here, on 2 June 1938,
the airman
Martin Haupt,
born 17 March 1914 in Meissen,
fell in the struggle for a national Spain"

Prelude to the bullfight in Castellon.

The Matador at the moment of delivering the fatal blow.

Mölders and Scholz during a visit to the front. A Spanish battalion commander explains the positions.

Scholz and Mölders with an artillery observer.

Nationalist tanks on their way to the front near Balaguer. (North Ebro offensive)

Burnt bodies in a Republican tank.

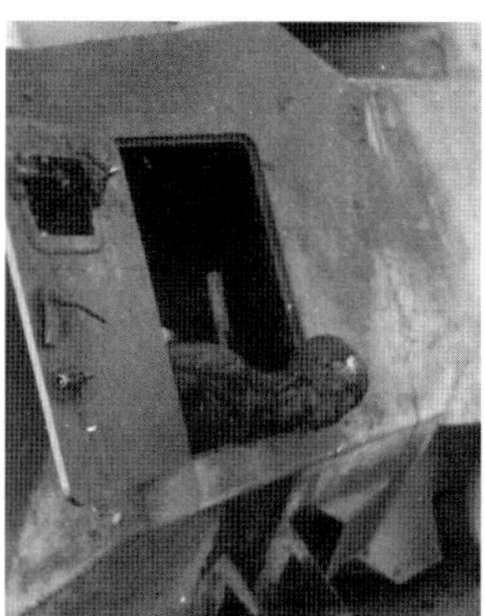

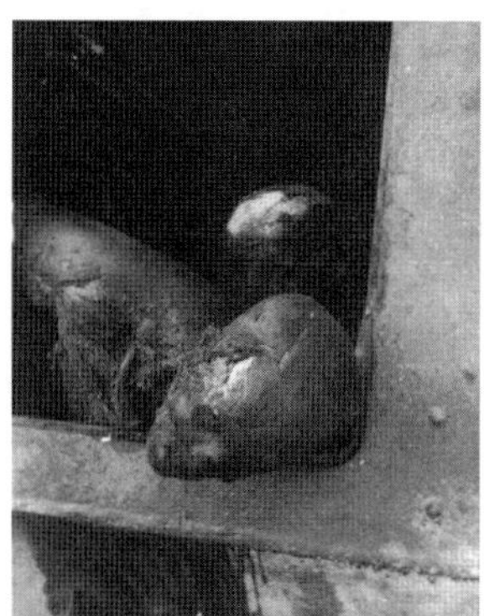

Visit to a battalion of the Spanish Foreign Legion with a four-hour lunch. Scholz is third from the left.

Moroccan soldiers stand guard on the beach.

German Me 109s over Spain. 6•51 is the aircraft of Wolfgang Schellmann.

Republican SB-2, the so-called "Martin Bomber". Designed and built in the Soviet Union, the aircraft caught fire easily when hit.

Red fighter, Polikarpov I-15.

He 59 maritime reconnaissance aircraft.

Ju 87 Stuka landing at La Cenia.

Werner Mölders after returning from a sortie.

Günther Scholz in Jesau, East Prussia in October 1938.

Scholz in his personal automobile (Hansa 1700 Sport, 6 cylinder) in front of the mess in Jesau.

Oberleutnant Wilhelm Balthasar at Buchenhöh Castle before the Sudeten operation in October 1938.

Departure from the castle for Mährisch-Trübau to inspect the airfield there (from left Balthasar, Scholz and Eggers).

Another photo of Wilhelm Balthasar taken during the Jagdgruppe's deployment to Jesau in 1938 (left Leutnant Mann).

Günther Scholz swing dancing with Walter Adolf (left).
Hauptmann Walter Adolf, Kommandeur of the II. Gruppe of Jagdgeschwader 26 "Schlageter", was awarded the Knight's Cross on 13 November 1940. By then he had scored sixteen victories, including one in Spain.

On 18 September 1941 Adolf was shot down during an engagement over the Channel. His body washed up on the Belgian coast three weeks later. At the time of his death, Walter Adolf's victory total stood at twenty-five.

The "Legion Condor" parade in Berlin, 6 June 1939.

The shields bearing the name of the German fallen in Spain.

Reviewing the formations.
From left: Adolf Hitler, Commander-in-Chief of the Navy Erich Raeder, Commander-in-Chief of the Air Force Hermann Göring and the three commanders of the "Legion Condor", Wolfram Freiherr von Richthofen, Helmuth Volkmann and Hugo Sperrle.

Closing parade with freshly-awarded decorations.

First day at the still-provisional air base at Gutenfeld near Königsberg. In the background are the private automobiles of the just-arrived pilots of the new Jagdgruppe.

Günther Scholz (left) during a flight briefing at Gutenfeld in August 1939.

Me 109s of the Jagdgruppe in flight over East Prussia.

Bore-sighting the machine-guns of a Me 109 D.

Gutenfeld, late August 1939. Seated in the right front seat is Oberleutnant Günther Scholz (with sunglasses). Behind him are Leutnant Heinz Lange (left) and Leutnant von Boeselager (right).

Günther Scholz at takeoff readiness at Gutenfeld just before the start of the war with Poland.

Scholz prepares for the Gruppe's first combat mission from Arys-Rostken against Warsaw on 1 September 1939.

I./JG 21's command post during the early days of the Polish campaign. On the left is the injured Gruppenkommandeur Major Mettig, to his right Staffelkapitän Scholz.

Briefing prior to another sortie. From left Major Mettig, Leutnant Rödel and Oberleutnant Eggers.

Günther Scholz and Gustav Rödel.

From left: Oberleutnant Günther Scholz, Leutnant Ernst Ewers and Leutnant Heinz Lange. All three were awarded the Iron Cross, First Class on 17 September 1939.

Hitler with his aides during lunch on 22 September 1939 during his trip to the front outside Warsaw.

Günther Scholz (left) during morning ablutions at Bialystok.

Bialystok airfield, late September 1939.

Waiting to hand the airfield over to the Russians. On the extreme left is Oberleutnant Scholz, fourth from the left Major Mettig, sixth from the left Leutnant Lange.

Oberleutnant Scholz's ground crew at Hopsten airfield in November 1939 (1./JG 21).

Leutnant Heinz Lange, also at Hopsten. The winged wooden shoe was the emblem of 1./JG 21.

Oberleutnant Günther Scholz in January 1940.

Two photographs taken during the Gruppe's stay in Münster, January 1940. They show Günther Scholz with Oberleutnant Leo Eggers (above right), the Staffelkapitän of 2./JG 21, and Oberleutnant Richard Hausmann (below right).

The three Staffelkapitäne of I./JG 21 shared a room in the Gruppe's comfortable quarters in Münster.

During the move to Mönchen-Gladbach on 28 January 1940, the aircraft became bogged down in the mud caused by heavy rains.

Farewell to Major Mettig (fourth from left).

*The pilots of I./JG 21 enjoy lunch together at Mönchen-Gladbach, early May 1940.
From far left: Leutnant Heinz Lange, Leutnant Max-Hellmuth Ostermann, Leutnant Erich Heinbockel, Leutnant Albrecht Drees.
At the head of the table: Schmidt (an official in the Gruppenstab), Hauptmann Fritz Ultsch, Oberleutnant Ekkehard Schelcher, Oberleutnant Günther Scholz.
Far right: Oberleutnant Joachim Strauß, Oberfeldwebel Neumann.
Inner seats: Oberleutnant Leo Eggers, Leutnant Ewald Baumgarten, Oberleutnant Herbert Büsse, Leutnant Siegfried Schmidt.*

Staffel party at Mönchen-Gladbach in March 1940. To the right of Staffelkapitän Günther Scholz (standing) are Leutnants Heinz Lange and Max-Hellmuth Ostermann.

Lange, Scholz and Ostermann on the evening of the Staffel party.

Like all the other members of the Staffel, Oberleutnant Scholz and Leutnant Lange also took part in the dancing.

The road from Ghent to Bruges, littered with abandoned French and Belgian equipment.

Morane fighters destroyed on the ground at Cambrai.

Countless French prisoners.

A captured French tank near St. Quentin.

Oberleutnant Scholz (left) and Leutnant Behrens inspect the captured tank.

June 1940, Staffelkapitän Günther Scholz with his special duties officer Oberleutnant d.R. Joachim Strauß.

Pilots of the 1. Staffel of JG 21 in Holland in July 1941, when the unit was serving in as the defense role. (3rd from the left is Oberleutnant Scholz, 6th from the left Leutnant Ostermann.)

A Citroen automobile captured in Rouen, bearing the emblem of the "Wooden Shoe Staffel".

Leutnant Ostermann makes himself comfortable in the car.

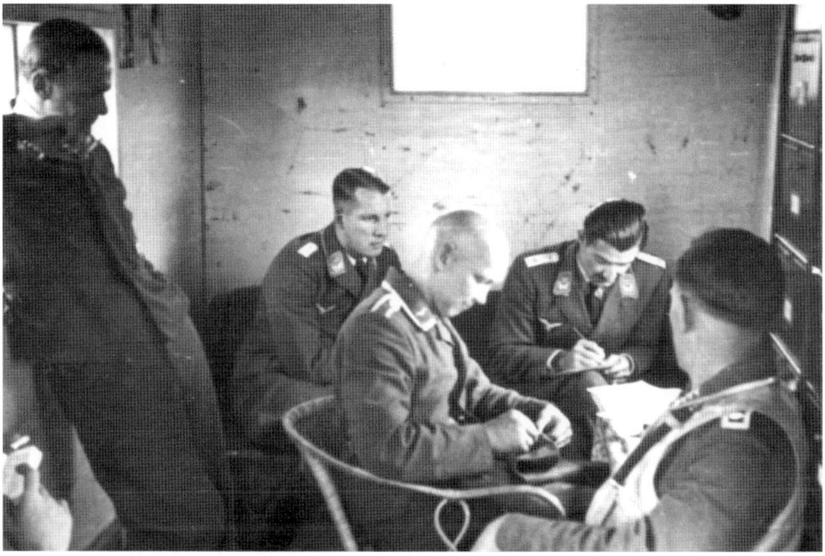

In the Staffel vehicle between missions. In the background are Leutnant Behrens (left) and Staffelkapitän Scholz.

The Staffelkapitän enjoying a game of chess.

Heinz Lange in 1945 as a Major and wearer of the Knight's Cross.

Another ground loop by Leutnant Ostermann at Guines.

The Gruppe positioned for takeoff from Guines airfield.

Personnel gather in front of the command post at Guines to watch the Gruppe take off on a mission over England.

This Armstrong-Whitworth Whitley Mk. V bomber of the RAF was shot down near Calais.

On 6 September 1940, I./JG 54 shot down this Spitfire, which made a forced landing. The aircraft was subsequently repaired.

Pilots relate their experiences after an air battle.

September 1940. Oberleutnant d.R. Joachim Strauß prepares for another mission over London. Born in 1899, he was one of the oldest fighter pilots at that time.

Günther Scholz in conversation with Hans-Ekkehard Bob (left).

Gathering of fighter pilots at Wissant in the command post of the Jafü 2. From left to right: Generalfeldmarschall Milch, Generalmajor von Döring (Jafü 2), Kommodore Major Trautloft.

An Me 109 with a bomb beneath the fuselage.

Front row:
Left Hauptmann Arnold Lignitz (Kommandeur of the III. Gruppe), right Hauptmann Dietrich Hrabak (Kommandeur of the II. Gruppe).

Back row, from left to right:
Oberleutnant Franz Eckerle (Kapitän of the 6. Staffel), Oberleutnant Hans-Ekkehard Bob (Kapitän of the 9. Staffel), Major Hannes Trautloft, Oberleutnant Hans Philipp (Kapitän of the 4. Staffel), Oberleutnant Richard Hausmann (Kapitän of the 8. Staffel) and Oberleutnant Günther Scholz (Kapitän of the 7. Staffel).

Even though the following two photos are somewhat blurry, they do give a good impression of the unforgettable Geschwader evening.

Kommodore Hannes Trautloft "knights" one of his pilots.

Oberleutnant Hans Ekkehard-Bob, Staffelkapitän of 9./JG 54.

The forward airfield at Pancevo. After the move from France to the outskirts of Belgrade, all of the pilots' baggage was removed from the motor caravan and each man had to search for his own cases. On witnessing these scenes, Leutnant Ostermann coined the phrase "Scholz's Traveling Circus". Present are all the officers of the 7. Staffel.

From left to right: Leutnant Max Clerico, Leutnant Gerhard Koall, Oberleutnant Günther Scholz, Leutnant Max-Hellmuth Ostermann, Leutnant Helmut Biederbick.

Pancevo forward airfield.

Oberleutnant Scholz and Leutnant Clerico.

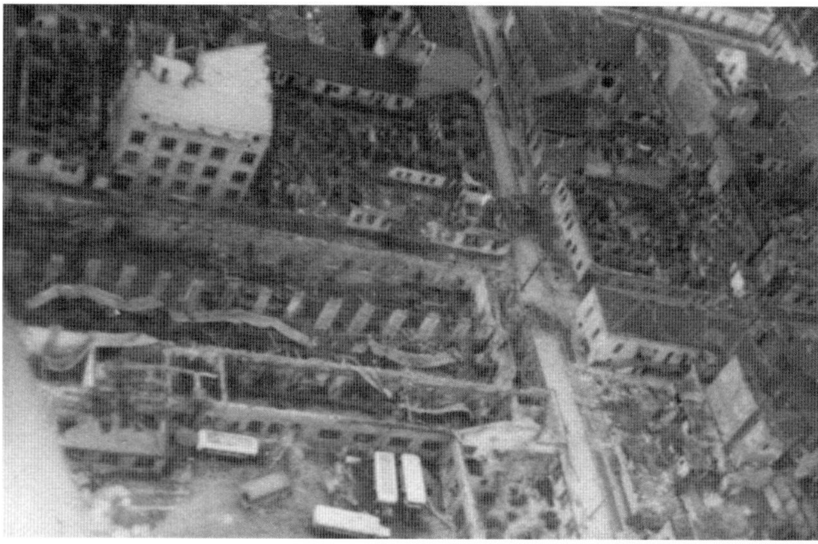

Aerial view of the wrecked city of Belgrade.

The big suspension bridge over the Danube between Belgrade and Semlin. Built by Germany after the First World War as a reparations payment, it was blown by during the Yugoslavian retreat.

Günther Scholz in Semlin near Belgrade.

Staffelkapitän Oberleutnant Scholz and Kommodore Major Trautloft brief Generaloberst Ernst Busch, the Commander-in-Chief of the 16th Army, on JG 54's successes.

Officers of 7./JG 54 enjoying lunch together. From left to right: Leutnant Gerhard Koall, Leutnant Hermann Leiste, Leutnant Helmut Biederbick, Leutnant Max-Hellmuth Ostermann, Oberleutnant Günther Scholz.

Inspecting Russian tanks knocked out on the Ostrov – Pskov road.

The 7. Staffel's tent camp at Ostrov-North. The men lived exclusively in tents until September. Tables and chairs were hand-made or brought along in the vehicles. For a time the paper war fell completely by the wayside. Bread and sugar were traded for sheep and pigs from the locals. The animals were then butchered and the meat supplemented the unit's diet.

The Staffel orderly office with Hauptfeldwebel Frey (center).

Bars representing the Staffel's victories were painted on the caravan. In July 1941, 7./JG 54 had 120 victories achieved over Belgium, France, England, Yugoslavia and Russia. By the end of the year the figure would be 270.

Kommodore Trautloft reading a report.

A later photo of Hannes Trautloft after promotion to Oberst.

Pilots of 7./JG 54
From left: Leutnant Peter Freiherr von Malapert, Leutnant Helmut Biederbick, Lt. Max-Hellmuth Ostermann, Lt. Hermann Leiste.

Hauptmann Arnold Lignitz (left) in Siverskaya with Oberleutnant Otto Kath, JG 54's adjutant, and Oberleutnant Spieß (right).

Oberleutnant Max-Hellmuth Ostermann after he was awarded the Knight's Cross with Swords.

Günther Scholz says goodbye to his comrades in JG 54. The photo was taken in Siverskaya on 7 February 1942.

Crossing the Arctic Circle.

The end of the railway in Rovaniemi, the capital city of Lapland.

Generaloberst Stumpff, the commander of Luftflotte 5, inspects the newly-arrived Jagdgruppe.

Inspecting the local area. Here Scholz is seen visiting an Orthodox monastery graveyard in Luostari. A number of graves were opened and washed away by flooding of the Petsamo-joki.

Geschwaderkommodore Handrick at the Gruppe command post.

Watching an air battle over Petsamo from the roof of the Gruppe command post.

Left Oberarzt Dr. Schulze-Gehrike.

Günther Scholz on the command post in Petsamo.

These two photos were taken during an air raid alert at 00:30 hours during the midnight sun in high summer. The pilots have left their quarters and await Russian aircraft in front of the slit trenches. They are wearing pajamas under their coats.

Another rest break interrupted by an air raid alarm.

In the shelter.

Generaloberst Stumpff, commander of Luftflotte 5, came to Petsamo for the awarding of the prestigious decoration. On the right is the freshly-decorated Feldwebel Müller, in the foreground his Gruppenkommandeur Hauptmann Horst Carganico. On the far left is the Kommandeur of the III. Gruppe, Hauptmann Günther Scholz.

This photo of Günther Scholz was also taken at the presentation ceremony of the Knight's Cross to Rudolf Müller. It provides an excellent view of the Spanish Cross in Gold with Swords.

A later photo of Rudolf Müller.

In July 1942 the Kommodore, Oberstleutnant Gotthard Handrick (right), addressed the two Gruppen of his Geschwader at Petsamo. On the left is the Kommandeur of the III. Gruppe, Hauptmann Günther Scholz. Standing behind Handrick is the Geschwader adjutant Hauptmann Brockmann.

Oberstleutnant Handrick and Hauptmann Brockmann.

Left: Staffelkapitän Hans-Curt von Sponeck reports to his Kommandeur Günther Scholz that his Staffel is assembled and ready for inspection.

Right: The two Gruppenkommandeure, Günther Scholz and Horst Carganico.

Right: Kommodore Handrick during his speech to the units. Behind him are Geschwader adjutant Brockmann (left) and Gruppenkommandeur Günther Scholz.

View of the assembled personnel of JG 5.

The Kommandeur receives the first congratulations while still in the cockpit.

His twenty-nine previous victories are marked on the tail of his aircraft.

Of course there has to be a vivid description of the combat. On Scholz's belt is the bottle of fly dope.

The Kommandeur in conversation with the Kapitän of his 8. Staffel, Oberleutnant Hermann Segatz.

When, on 30 December 1941, Oberleutnant Hermann Segatz assumed command of the Staffel that would later become 8./JG 5, he had eighteen victories to his credit, including eight against British fighter aircraft.
For his actions on the Polar Sea Front, on 25 September 1942 he was awarded the German Cross in Gold. At the beginning of June 1943 Segatz relinquished command of 8./JG 5 and became adjutant of the III. Gruppe.
After his promotion to Hauptmann, in February 1944 he took over command of II./JG 1. His new area of operations was the so-called Defense of the Reich. Segatz shot down seven American bombers in a few days, before he was himself shot down and killed on 8 March 1944. Hermann Segatz achieved a total of forty confirmed victories.

Oberleutnant Rudolf Lüder, the III. Gruppe's adjutant, returns from another sortie.

Waiting for the others to return. On the far left is the tail of Günther Scholz's machine, now with thirty victory bars.

Oberleutnant Rudolf Lüder in conversation with the III. Gruppe's technical officer, Leutnant Friedrich Schumann.

Oberleutnant Rudolf Lüder and Hauptmann Hans-Curt von Sponeck.

In August 1942 Kommandeur Günther Scholz and his Staffelkapitän Hans-Curt von Sponeck visited the main line of resistance held by the mountain troops, where they were shown the Russian positions.

Feldwebel Heinrich Bartels is presented the Knight's Cross awarded to him on 13 November 1942. On the left is Oberst Alexander Holle, the Fliegerführer Nord (Ost), on the right Gruppenkommandeur Hauptmann Günther Scholz.

The feats of the ground personnel in the cold winter months were unimaginable. The actions by these mainly anonymous personnel cannot be remembered often enough.

Hauptmann Günther Scholz and Oberleutnant Hermann Segatz watch Russian fighters over Petsamo.

Kommodore Oberstleutnant Gotthard Handrick in the cockpit of his aircraft.

Supplies for the German mountain troops at the front before Murmansk were delivered by reindeer columns.

The moose shot from the Fieseler Storch were butchered on the spot. From left: Oberleutnant Moeck, Hauptmann Hans von Hahn of the Geschwaderstab and Oberleutnant Bernhard Probst, JG 5's technical officer.

Mess and headquarters barracks in Petsamo, winter 1942-43.

Christmas 1942 in Petsamo. In response to a shortage of Christmas tree decorations, long metal strips were turned on a lathe and used to decorate the tree. The effect was outstanding.

Günther Scholz in the officer's mess.

The long-distance wedding of Oberleutnant Wulf-Dietrich Widowitz.

Front right Oberleutnant Widowitz, behind him Oberleutnant Segatz, third from left Stabsintendant Berkefeld.

After the ceremony the participants celebrated together.

The Fliegerführer Nord (Ost), Generalmajor Alexander Holle, inspects the newly-created Jabostaffel, 14./JG 5 under Hauptmann Friedrich-Wilhelm Strakeljahn, at Petsamo.

Generalmajor Alexander Holle in conversation with a pilot of the new Jabostaffel. Behind him is the Kommandeur of III./JG 5, Hauptmann Günther Scholz, and right Friedrich-Wilhelm Strakeljahn, Staffelkapitän of 14./JG 5.

Friedrich-Wilhelm Strakeljahn, born on 7 September 1914, had been a member of the Luftwaffe since 1935. When the war broke out, he was the Gruppenkommandeur of I.(J)/LG 2. On 20 May 1940 he became Kapitän of the Gruppe's 2. Staffel. During the Western Campaign he amassed a great deal of experience in fighter-bomber operations and shot down five enemy aircraft.

In July 1942 he assumed command of 12./JG 5. Hauptmann Strakeljahn was awarded the German Cross in Gold on 21 September 1942. He took over JG 5's Jabostaffel at the end of March 1943. In recognition of the unit's success, he was awarded the Knight's Cross on 19 August. Strakeljahn was later killed near Dvinsk on 6 July 1944 as Kommandeur of II./SG 4.

The personnel of III./JG in formation in Petsamo on 20 April 1943.

The Kommandeur decorates deserving personnel of his Jagdgruppe.

Return from a combat mission.

In Petsamo the ground is slowly thawing out again.

In his role as Gruppenkommandeur, Scholz performs another long-distance wedding for one of his men.

Günther Scholz in the cockpit of his Me 109 before take off.

Günther Scholz was promoted to Major on 1 April 1943.

The following photographs were taken during a visit to Petsamo by Generaloberst Eduard Dietl, Commander-in-Chief of the 20th Army, the so-called Lapland Army. Dietl was accompanied by the commanding general of the XIX Mountain Corps, General der Gebirgstruppen Ferdinand Schörner.

Also present to welcome the high-ranking visitors were the Fliegerführer Nord (Ost), Generalmajor Alexander Holle, and the commander of the Petsamo air base, Oberstleutnant Arthur van Aaken. They may be seen in the above photo, accompanied by Major Günther Scholz.

Generalmajor Holle in conversation with General Schörner.

Generalmajor Holle in conversation with Generaloberst Dietl.

Major Günther Scholz and Oberstleutnant Arthur van Aaken.

General der Gebirgstruppen Ferdinand Schörner (left) and Generaloberst Eduard Dietl.

The new leader of JG 5, Major Günther Scholz, and the new Kommandeur of III./JG 5, Hauptmann Heinrich Ehrler.

A visit to Mountain Regiment 139 is used to go riding.

Günther Scholz as a Major wearing the German Cross in Gold and the Spanish Cross in Gold with Swords.

Günther Scholz before a mission against an American convoy north of Murmansk.

Major Scholz and Stabsintendant Berkefeld.

Midday break in front of the headquarters barracks in Petsamo.

These photographs were taken on the day of the change of command in the position of Fliegerführer Nord (Ost) in August 1943. From left: an unidentified Oberst, Oberst d.R. Dr. Ernst Kühl, operations officer Major Ehlers, Major Günther Scholz and Generalmajor Ernst-August Roth.

Theodor Weißenberger as a Leutnant in a blast pen during his days with 6./JG 5.

Another photo of Theodor Weißenberger. It shows him as an Oberleutnant and wearer of the Knight's Cross of the Iron Cross with Oak Leaves.

This photo of Josef Kammhuber was taken in 1941 and shows him as a Generalmajor.

Günther Scholz and members of his staff on the terrace of his villa in Stavanger-Gausel.

Hauptmann Probst (left) and Stabsintendant Berkefeld on the terrace.

View of the Gams Fjord.

Conversation on the terrace. From left: Hauptmann Probst, Hauptmann Schmidt and Oberstleutnant Scholz.

Scholz in his staff car.

A pleasant coffee break.

Günther Scholz and Bernhard Probst on the terrace of the villa in Stavanger-Gausel on a Sunday afternoon.

In this photo Heinrich Ehrler is a Hauptmann wearing the Knight's Cross.

Walter Schuck, the third member of JG 5 to surpass the mark of 200 victories.

The staff of the Jagdfliegerführer Norwegen during firearms practice in the spring of 1945. In the middle is Oberstleutnant Scholz.

The final photographs, taken on 8 May 1945, the day of the German surrender.